Point of Purchase
DESIGN

Point of Purchase
DESIGN

**The Graphics of
Merchandise Display**

Robert B. Konikow

PBC International, Inc., New York, New York

Distributors to the trade in the United States:
Robert Silver Associates
95 Madison Avenue
New York, NY 10016

Distributors to the trade in Canada:
General Publishing Co. Ltd.
30 Lesmill Road
Don Mills, Ontario, Canada M3B 2T6

Distributed in continental Europe by:
Feffer and Simons, B.V.
170 Rijnkade
Weesp, Netherlands

Distributed throughout the rest of the world by:
Fleetbooks, S.A.
℅ Feffer and Simons, Inc.
100 Park Avenue
New York, NY 10017

Library of Congress Cataloging in Publication Data

Konikow, Robert B.
   Point of purchase design.

   Includes indexes.
   1. Advertising, Point-of-sale.   2. Display of merchandise.   I. Title
HF5845.K72   1984   659.1'57   84-19036
ISBN 0-86636-003-4

Color separation, printing, and binding by
Toppan Printing Co. (H.K.) Ltd., Hong Kong

Typesetting by **Trufont Typographers, Inc.**
Hicksville, New York

Printed in Hong Kong

10 9 8 7 6 5 4 3 2 1

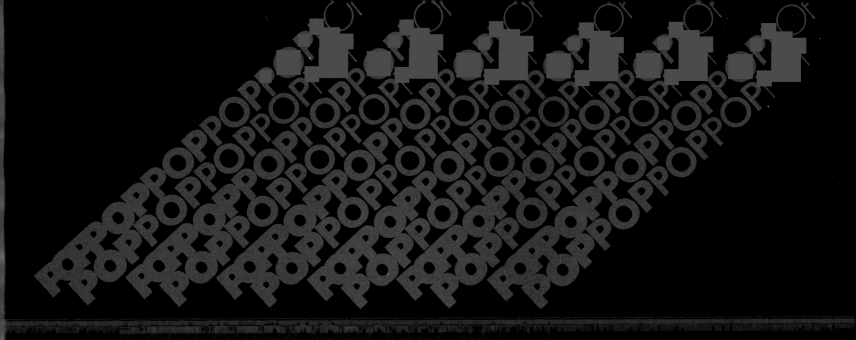

publisher:	Herb Taylor
project director:	Cora S. Taylor
editors:	Carol Denby
	Linda Weinraub
art director:	Richard Liu
art associates:	Charlene Sison
	Dan Kouw

Contents

Foreword

Literally hundreds of books have been written about the communications business. Books about advertising, books about sales promotion, books about direct mail, books about premiums—with special segments within the many disciplines accounting for many more. Very few have been published about one of our most dynamic mediums—Point of Purchase—and I know of none dedicated to the design of P.O.P.

Bob Konikow has put together such a book. It has been a monumental task because the medium is so diverse. That very diversity is what makes this book of immense value to all of us engaged in the business of selling our wares where the majority of buying decisions are really made—at the point of purchase.

The word "design" includes so many elements it is difficult, if not impossible, to define. We know it includes vital input from the advertiser. It may be necessary to incorporate elements from print or electronic campaigns to create that all-important synergistic impact. Budgets always impose limitations. Placement locations, channels, and methods of distribution play a part. All these factors influence the choice of materials and engineering and reproduction techniques which are applicable within the budget.

It has always been my premise that any damn fool can be creative on an unlimited budget. Real creativity is only evidenced when a superior point-of-purchase product is produced in the quantity required—and within the budget.

Good design is, of course, based on knowledge and experience. And that is not the limited knowledge that one individual can accumulate even in a lifetime in the business — it is the knowledge that we gain in observing the good works of our peers and adapting good ideas, good graphics, good construction and material utilization, good engineering, and good common sense to meet our objectives.

Creativity is 0b percent memory. Some may object to this statement, but nearly 40 years in the business make me believe it.

This is really what *Point of Purchase Design* is all about. It's a collection of displays and signage—of design—that has worked. It provides an immediate opportunity and a continuing source of information, of review, and of comparison for almost every conceivable utilization of the point-of-purchase medium. It's a daily memory jogger for creativity.

Point of Purchase Design is a valuable addition to the library of almost everyone engaged in marketing communications. Advertisers and agencies alike will benefit from looking and learning.

J. J. BURLINGAME
Director of Sales Promotion
Dow Chemical USA
Midland Michigan

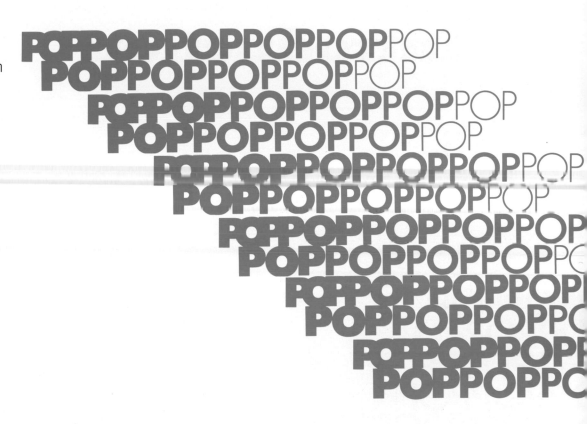

Introduction

POPPOPPOP
OPPOPPOP
POPPOPPOPPOP
OPPOPPOPPOP
OPPOPPOPPOPPOP
PPOPPOPPOPPOP
OPPOPPOPPOPPOPPOP
POPPOPPOPPOPPOP
POPPOPPOPPOPPOPPOP
POPPOPPOPPOPPOP
POPPOPPOPPOPPOPPOP
POPPOPPOPPOPPOP

What is point-of-purchase advertising?

It is difficult to generalize about this dynamic medium. If you were to leaf through this book without prior experience with the medium, you would probably find it difficult to decide what these hundreds of objects have in common, and what it is they share that make them eligible for inclusion.

It isn't size, since they vary from objects small enough to be hidden by the hand to those that fill a wall. It isn't material, since almost every conceivable substance may be used, from sheets of paper to wood or metal or plastic. It certainly isn't the nature of the advertiser, for the medium is used for almost every category of product.

The key lies in its name. What all of the units pictured here have in common is that they are designed to be used at the point where the purchase can be made, where interest in the product can be turned immediately into action, where desire can be changed into fulfillment, and where the end result is satisfaction.

Because point-of-purchase advertising is so flexible and so varied, its producers are free to experiment. A newspaper or magazine ad must be designed to fit the limitations of the printing press; a television ad ends up on film or tape; but point-of-purchase advertising, since it is self-contained, is limited only by the ingenuity of its designer and by the economics of the market. Of all the media, it is the first to be able to adopt new technological advances.

For that reason, it is considered a new, modern, medium. But in fact, it is one of the oldest media of commercial communication. As soon as society began to develop, as soon as specialists began to arrive on the scene, there developed a need for a way to let people know where they could obtain specific products. The division of labor forced the man who made shoes for a living to indicate that his house or shop was where others could come to trade their goods or services for his shoes. Perhaps the shoemaker first stationed somebody outside his door to call out his wares, but soon a sign, painted or carved, on the front of the house, told the same story at less cost. Since most people were illiterate, these signs used pictures to tell their message. A gloved hand for a glover, a bunch of grapes for a vintner, were typical. Signs like these were uncovered in the ruins of ancient Pompeii.

The next step was to paint these pictures on slabs of wood, and hang them at right angles to the wall, so they could be seen from a distance. Taverns in England used this kind of sign, often with very elaborate symbolism, and they are still in use. Other signs were three-dimensional. A carved boot or a fully shaped head of a hog made clear the nature of the business within. The Medici's cost of arms contained three golden balls, and this symbol, translated into three dimensions, still indicates a pawnbroker,

the inheritor of the Medici tradition. The red-and-white pole which we recognize as the sign of the barber derives from the early function of this tradesman, then a barber/surgeon whose main therapeutic technique was bloodletting.

In its physical aspects, point-of-purchase advertising is more varied than any other advertising medium.

Television, today's dominant medium if you measure dominance by money invested or by the number of impressions, offers an exciting combination of pictures that move, bright colors, music, voice, and sound effects, as well as a choice of photographic and animation techniques. It is a tremendously creative medium, with almost infinite possibilities, but it all ends up as a reel of motion picture film or videotape which appears on a rectangular screen in the home. And the production cost is high.

Newspaper and magazine ads offer great creative scope, too, but with few exceptions they end up as words and illustrations printed on a piece of flat paper and distributed as part of a publication.

Direct mail adds the possibility of unusual die-cutting and folding, as well as the use of three-dimensional objects, and can thus be more varied and often more exciting. But it must still conform to postal regulations and be suitable for these distribution channels.

Outdoor advertising, via billboards, is often used close to the point of purchase, but it is essentially flat, although some attempts at a third dimension have been attempted. Because of mechanical

limitations, it is used in a few standardized sets of dimensions.

Point-of-purchase advertising, however, is almost entirely free of physical limitations. It can cover the whole gamut of physical size from a small decal that goes on a store window to a massive rotating sign in a service station that requires a crane and a crew of construction workers for installation.

A point-of-purchase display can be flat, in bas-relief, or in full round sculpture. It can be intended for use indoors or outdoors. It can be designed to stand on the floor, on a table or counter, attached to a wall, or hung from a ceiling. It can utilize every technique to reach people through any of their senses—color, light, motion, sound, touch, and even scent—to attract attention and to help convey its message.

The unifying factor that makes point-of-purchase a single entity, that gives it a unity, is simply its location. Any advertising medium that is placed at or near the place where the purchase is made automatically falls into the point-of-purchase category. Its placement is what counts, and the development of how to do this most effectively at this crucial point in the chain that leads to the buying decision is the factor which has brought together the wide variety of skills and crafts that may be seen at any of the annual POPAI exhibits, or the examples of the designers' skills represented in this volume.

The Role of the Designer

Behind every project shown in this book, or indeed, every project seen in the commercial world, there is at least one designer. Each of these structures—of varied materials, vivid colors, extraordinary conformations, and eye-catching impact—started out as an idea.

A client asks for a display that will accomplish a specific objective in relation to a specific product. He imposes certain conditions, including an estimate of the number needed and an approximate budget, and probably a time schedule. The designer then draws on his experience to develop a proposed display that will meet all the requirements.

Unfortunately, some of the requirements are contradictory. Certain features that might be included to increase the attention-value of a display, for example, may raise the unit cost beyond the level permitted by the budget. The time schedule may be too tight to permit the acquisition of a special material that is not readily available. Perhaps the cost can be reduced by using a stock extrusion rather than a custom one; if this is possible, would the change reduce the effectiveness of the finished display?

The designer must draw on his experience for the solutions to these problems. Utilizing what he has learned, he comes up first with a sketch, and later with a working drawing, that will balance all these considerations, resulting in a display that helps the client achieve his objectives.

The designer is, of course, an artist. He must be able to have ideas and transfer them to paper. He must be able to present his concepts in a manner that is understandable to a client, who may very well have a limited visual imagination. He must understand enough of human nature to know how to add appeal to a design. He must have some background in the industry for which he is working, to know what is acceptable in each kind of outlet in which displays are used. As can be readily seen in the pages of this book, the type of display designed to sell food in a crowded supermarket would not be appropriate in a fine jewelry store. Displays, even for the identical product, must fit the environment for which they are intended. A lipstick display for a supermarket shelf would not be acceptable for the counter of a department store.

Finally, a designer must know his materials and their production limitations. He must know what can and cannot be done with paper and cardboard, with wood and plastic, with wire and metal extrusions. He must know how displays are shipped and assembled, and how to estimate, from his early drawings, what the cost of production will be. He must know how to include light, motion, and other characteristics that will make his display compelling and unique.

Working with point-of-purchase displays is a challenge for a designer, since it is a constantly changing field. Not only are new materials continually becoming available, but price ratios are never constant. What was impractical yesterday is eminently within reach today. Yesterday's dreams are today's possibilities.

The Process of Creativity

Point-of-purchase advertising is a demanding medium, and it requires imagination and creativity from its very beginning. The client must start it off with a clear definition of his objective, and a realistic look at his position in the market and what is within reaching distance. He must remember that the use of a point-of-purchase display depends on its acceptance by the retailer, who must be convinced that the benefits he will realize by its use will outweigh his investment of time and money. He must be convinced that the display will add to his bottom line, and not merely shift sales from one brand to another.

After the objective, which must be defined by, or at least be acceptable to the client, comes the concept. This certainly includes the theme, and often the headline and the copy. This is usually supplied by the client's agency—occasionally his advertising agency, often his sales promotion agency, frequently his point-of-purchase agency.

With this in hand, and backed up with a budget, the designer can go to work. Depending upon the way in which his company is structured, and on his own personal background and experience, he may be responsible for both the appearance and the physical structure of the display, but often the design is a collaborative effort.

It starts out as a sketch, sometimes a very elaborate and detailed one. Some clients need and demand a model. Once approval has been granted, it moves into finished artwork on one hand and production drawings on the other. In addition to cost restrictions, the designer is faced with the problem of ease of shipping and setting up. He may also be involved in preparing materials to help sell the display to retailers.

It sounds complicated, and it is, but it is a process that works well hundreds of times a year, as the displays included in this volume indicate. All the displays you see here have faced the real world, have achieved success, and have gained recognition from those who use this immediate marketing medium. We hope that their inclusion here will help the industry increase its efficiency.

A Note on OMA

A number of the displays included in this book include the note "OMA winner," and we owe the reader a word of explanation about OMA and what it means. The initials stand for "Outstanding Merchandising Award," which is given each year to display units in a competition sponsored by the Point-of-Purchase Advertising Institute, better known as POPAI (and which we would like to thank for its help in producing this volume).

The competition, the most prestigious in the industry, has been held annually since 1960, and although there have been minor changes in the procedures and categories, the most recent rules of the competition are remarkably like the earliest.

Most of the entries—and most years there have been between 1,000 and 2,000 of them!—are submitted by producer members of POPAI. Each is assigned to its industrial category, and the judging is done within these categories. Advertiser members of POPAI may enter any displays they have sponsored, whether or not they have been produced by a POPAI member.

For the final judging, the actual display is set up, so that the judges base their scoring on the real thing, not on a photograph or drawing of the unit. No judge is asked to score more than a fraction of the total entries, and producers of displays are not permitted to be on the

judging teams, each of which consists of three representatives from national and regional advertisers, judging outside their own industry. Producer members of POPAI are not permitted to serve on a judging team.

Four criteria are set out for the guidance of the judges:

1. Effectiveness of the unit as a solution to the requirements set forth in the case history.
2. Originality of concept
3. Quality of reproduction and/or manufacture.

Bronze OMA statuettes are awarded to the advertisers and producers of those displays which are judged outstanding in their merchandising categories. Silver awards are presented to the top-scoring entry in each type of point-of-purchase unit, ranging from floor stands and clocks to merchandisers and testers. Gold OMAs are presented to those displays receiving Best of Marketplace awards, for accomplishments in advertising, selling, merchandising, or incentive programs and promotions. And finally, a blue ribbon panel of marketing executives selects the Display-of-the-Year from the winners of the Gold OMA.

POPPOPPOPPOP
POPPOPPOPPOPPOP
POPPOPPOPPOPPOP
POPPOPPOPPOPPOP
POPPOPPOPPOPPOP
POPPOPPOPPOPPOP
POPPOPPOPPOPPOP
POPPOPPOPPOPPOP
POPPOPPOPPOPPOP
POPPOPPOPPOI

1

Health and Beauty Aids

Display designers for the products included in this category face a set of challenges that are perhaps unmatched by any other category. This is especially true of units that are produced for cosmetics and fragrances.

The major challenge is to make a unit that is strong enough and dominating enough to catch the eye of the passer-by, and yet one that is subordinate to the decor of the store in which it is to be used. For cosmetics in the upper price range, whose chief outlets are fine department stores and, to some extent, up-grade pharmacies, this becomes a major contradiction that must be solved by the designer. These stores are proud of their identities, and do not wish to be dominated by any brand except, perhaps, their own. They will refuse to accept displays that seem to conflict with the store decor. And yet to stand out in the glittering store milieu, some element of conflict must be introduced.

Two other concerns also guide the designer of displays in this product category. Most cosmetic lines come in a bewildering variety of colors, and selection is very important to the customer. So while the containers for lipsticks or for nail polishes may look very much alike, the customer has very specific wishes, and wants to be sure that she has made the proper selection. Add to this the desire for sampling, and a further complication is introduced that affects the design of the display.

The other concern is the common one of pilferage. Cosmetics, like jewelry, are among the most common targets of shoplifters. The threat is greatest, of course, in mass-merchandise outlets, where there are likely to be fewer store personnel on hand. Again, there is the conflict between access and security.

In this chapter you will see some very elegant solutions to these problems.

Over-the-counter drug items fall into two groups. The most visible is made up of widely used materials, generally supported by heavy advertising in print and on the air. The approach here is very similar to that used in supermarkets, where almost anything goes to attract attention, where the atmosphere is very competitive and boldness is virtually a necessity.

Less familiar products, or those less active, need a different kind of display. They have to say more than "Here I am!"

The displays must be able to pick out from the total customer population those to whom the product has meaning, and then explain the product's function. And since the volume on these items is necessarily small, the product managers must convince store management that the display is worth the space it occupies. This sub-group may well offer the display designer their most difficult challenge, and yet, as can be seen from some of the examples in this chapter, it is not an insoluble problem.

ADVERTISER: Niki de Saint Ralle
PRODUCER: Ledan Inc.

The small spray tester is given prominence and significance by this impressive holder, with its clear plastic base and its heavy gold-embossed top.

ADVERTISER: Stetson, Coty Inc.
Joseph Palamara, Director of Display Development
PRODUCER: Trans World Manufacturing Corp.

Appealing to the up-scale executive with its fine illustration and elegant design, this unit offers special travel size units at a special price, tucked away in an attaché-case-like drawer in the base of the display. Bronze OMA 1983.

ADVERTISER: Zizanie, Jovan Inc.
Donald Deegan, VP & General Manager, Vitabath Inc.
Michael Westhusing, Packaging
PRODUCER: Patrick H. Joyce and Associates

A shallow display was developed to introduce a new product. It contains an assortment of products, and a tester in the center. The header can be removed, if necessary, for shelf installation. Bronze OMA 1983.

ADVERTISER: Guerlain Inc.
Rozanne Isney, Sales Promotion Manager
PRODUCER: Trans World Manufacturing Corp.

Destined for top department stores and better drug stores, this display had to compete with many other high-ticket cosmetics. The simple, classic design uses black opaque and mirrored plexi. Each of the three bottles is a tester. Bronze OMA 1983.

ADVERTISER: Maybelline Cosmetics, Plough Inc.
Gary Howerton, Assistant Display Manager
Robert Maxwell, Display Manager
PRODUCER: Trans World Manufacturing Corp.

This very pretty display provided an elegant and romantic image for the promotion of scented stationery as a premium, and was very appropriate for suggesting Mother's Day gift purchases. Bronze OMA 1983.

ADVERTISER: Max Factor and Company
Greg Bachelor, Display Director
PRODUCER: Dauman Displays Inc.
Sid Dauman, Designer

This compact unit permits the customer to sample any one (or all) of the fragrances simply by placing her hand on the paddle eliminating the problem of stolen sample bottles. The photographs of the bottles, in full color, are processed on foil to simulate a glow of the product. Silver OMA 1983.

ADVERTISER: Max Factor & Co.
Greg Bachelor, Display Director
PRODUCER: Display Systems Inc.

Used during the initial introduction of a new product, prior to the beginning of an advertising program, the display had to enhance the product and impress the retailers. This was achieved with the development of a wicker, lined, garden basket, made out of white vacuum-formed plastic. Four counter displays, below, were designed to get crucial counter space during the Christmas season. Bronze OMA 1983.

ADVERTISER: Coparel
PRODUCER: Creative Displays Inc.

This two-tiered counter display, formed from a single piece of smoky plastic, lets the package be the star.

ADVERTISER: Elizabeth Arden
Julie Salzberg, Package Development Associate
PRODUCER: Trans World Manufacturing Corp.

The elegance of the mirrored fans capitalizes on the shape of the containers, and reminds the consumer that the product is from Lagerfeld, whose trademark is a fan. Bronze OMA 1983.

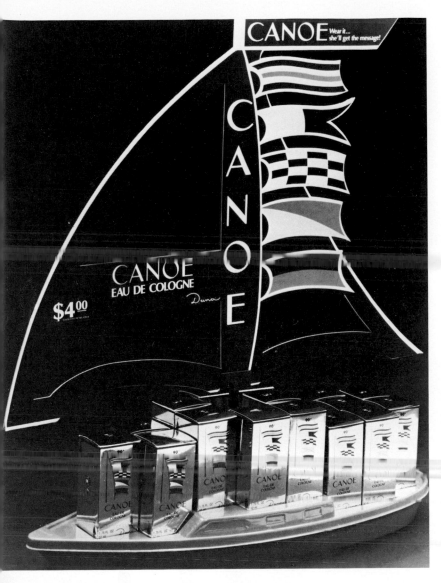

ADVERTISER: Canoe, Dana Corporation
PRODUCER: Immco Displays Inc.

This sail boat counter merchandiser offers a contrast to the more rectangular units. Its sails are die-cut to avoid blocking off counter area. The graphic risers pick up the art on the packages. Bronze OMA 1983.

ADVERTISER: Yardley of London, Jovan Inc.
Michael Westhusing, Packaging Specialist
PRODUCER: Patrick H. Joyce & Associates
Hal Nickel, Designer

This corrugated display suggested the garden feeling of the product, offering easy-to-take gift products.

ADVERTISER: Omni Cosmetics Corp. Jovan
Donald P. Deegan
PRODUCER: Patrick H. Joyce & Associates Inc.
Hal Nickel, Designer

Used to introduce the product line, the robot, with its vacuum-formed dome, succeeded in attracting attention to the products it held. Bronze OMA award 1982.

ADVERTISER: Omni Cosmetics Corp., Jovan Inc.
Donald P. Deegan VP & General Manager
Michael Westhusing, Packaging Specialist
PRODUCER: Patrick H. Joyce & Associates Inc.

This red and black display holds as many as 80 product packages. Bronze OMA award.

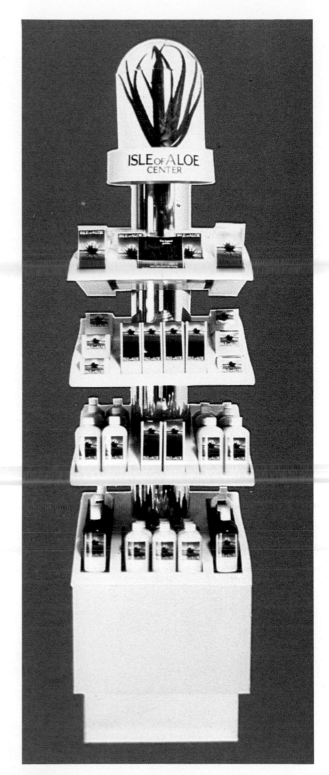

ADVERTISER: Le Jardin fragrance, Max Factor & Co.
Gregory G. Bachelor, Director of Display
PRODUCER: Acorn Display

A summer atmosphere is suggested by the lattice-work side panels, with two shelves for ample product presentation. Made of corrugated and foamboard, with a litho full-color photograph to tie in with the advertising.

ADVERTISER: Isle of Aloe
Rich Davidian, Group Marketing Director, New Products
PRODUCER: The Howard/Marlboro Group
Milton Merl, Designer

The total line of this new product can be set up on this display in a unified way, setting it apart from similar products found on gondola shelves.

ADVERTISER: Dimension, Lever Brothers Co.
Edward J. Sinusas Jr. Purchasing Agent, Printing and Displays
Eugene C. Marotta, Marketing Manager
PRODUCER: Henschel-Steinau Inc.

This pre-packed counter display holds six of the four sizes in the line, backed up by a brilliant riser card that ties in with the product's advertising. Bronze OMA award.

ADVERTISER: Aziza, Chesebrough Ponds Inc.
Donald Scheiber, Purchasing Agent
Mary Ann Pettorini, Art Director
PRODUCER: POP Displays Inc.

The customer is invited to demonstrate a new eyeshadow by using the attached pencil and sharpener. The product tray has 10 glued-in pencils to illustrate colors. This tray can be easily removed for replacement when necessary, and to give sales people access to the stock kept inside. Bronze OMA 1983.

ADVERTISER: Impulse, Lever Brothers Co.
Edward Sinusas, Buyer
PRODUCER: Displayco East
Dennis Claussen, Designer

Designed to introduce a new product with a trial size offer, this unit was shipped as a pre-pack for easy assembly. The trays can be removed and used as shelf organizers or counter displays.

ADVERTISER: Liquid Ivory, Procter and Gamble
Dutro Blocksom, Art Director
PRODUCER: Henschel-Steinau

The product is available on all sides from three compartmentalized trays supported by fiber tubes. The angling of the base, which protects the stand from floor mops, adds interest. Bronze OMA 1983.

ADVERTISER: Jovan Inc.
Joseph P. Forkish, VP and General Manager
PRODUCER: Dauman Displays Inc.
Sid Dauman, Designer

This counter unit is a new concept in testing fragrances. The customer simply places his or her hand on the graphics, and a small amount of fragrance is sprayed on the hand. The product is on the top of the unit, for easy access without the help of a sales person. The unit has proved to be especially helpful in getting reluctant males to test a fragrance. The header can be replaced for different products and promotions. Bronze OMA 1983.

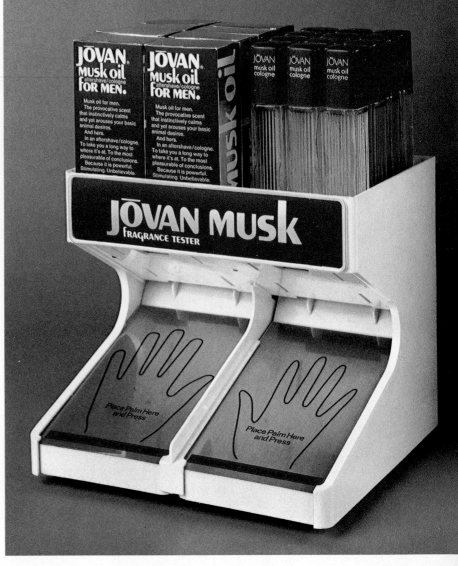

ADVERTISER: Revlon Inc.
Carmine Parisi, Purchasing Director
PRODUCER: Display Producers Inc.

The large head of the attractive woman, staring almost daringly ahead, grabs the eye of the passerby in almost any store environment. Continuing right into the product area, it leads the eye to the goods. The variety of products in the new colors tends to increase the volume of each sale.

ADVERTISER: Impulse, Lever Brothers Co.
Edward Sinusas, Buyer
Herman Pizzi, Designer
PRODUCER: Displayco East

This clean, sleek-looking floor stand was aimed to reach the 15–21 year old female market. The tray makes it easy for the customer to pick out a bottle, and is easy to refill because of the individual holders for each.

ADVERTISER: Chaps, Warner Cosmetics Inc.
Roberta Dinerstein, Director of Marketing
Chris Rocace, Director of Package Development
PRODUCER: Nadelson Displays Inc.

The flavor of the Old West is depicted in this counter display, made of raw wood with a brown product platform. Bronze OMA award.

ADVERTISER: la Solaire, Schering-Plough Inc.
Robert Maxwell, Display Manager
Ted Kingsford, VP, Marketing
PRODUCER: Trans World Manufacturing Corp.

Beauty, warmth and prestige were the goals of this floorstand. Its design picks up the colors and graphics of the package, and turns it into an elegant tower with two trays of products. Bronze OMA 1983.

ADVERTISER: Clairesse, Clairol Inc.
Robert Stadda, Manager of Display and Promotion Group
Jeff Rafalaf, Art Director
PRODUCER: Henschel-Steinau Inc.

These trays are designed to lock together, using tabs that are molded as part of the units. In addition, the retailer can break off rear sections if necessary to suit the depth of a shelf. Samples of hair pieces for each color add pull to the display, and satisfy customers' needs to see the real color. Bronze OMA 1983.

ADVERTISER: L'Oreal Inc.
Bill Lush, Promotional Purchasing Manager
PRODUCER: Dauman Displays Inc.
Sid Dauman, Designer

To add flexibility to its program, this unit was constructed with telescoping metal side sections and headers, so it will fit any height and width from 3–8 feet. It can easily be installed into existing pegboard walls. Its internal components of injection-molded styrene and wire hooks are removable and replaceable, to adapt to changing product lines. Silver OMA 1983.

ADVERTISER: Yardley and Company Ltd.
Bob Betteley, Merchandising Manager
PRODUCER: Dauman Displays Inc.
Sid Dauman, Designer

This wall unit, which prominently carries the brand name, is designed so that all interior components are movable to accommodate changes in the product line. Bronze OMA 1983.

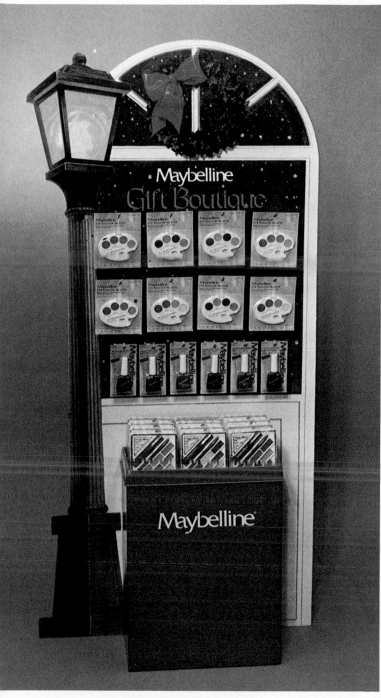

ADVERTISER: Mary Quant Cosmetics, Max Factor & Co.
Robert Lee, Merchandise Manager
PRODUCER: PD Visual Marketing Ltd.
Dinesh Mistry and Philip Osborne, Designers

This permanent unit, with its cantilevered shelves, carries a complete line of products. The more expensive items can be displayed in the enclosed case, while the locked cabinet is used for storage. Bronze OMA 1983.

ADVERTISER: Maybelline, Schering Plough Inc.
Ted Kingsford, VP, Marketing Services
Robert Maxwell, Display Development Manager
Gary Howerton, Asst. Display Development Manager
PRODUCER: Displayco East
Grace Akillian, Designer

This floorstand was designed to take advantage of high traffic levels during the holiday season. Simply by changing graphics, it can be used for a variety of theme promotions throughout the year.

ADVERTISER: Coty Inc.
Joseph Palamara, Display Development Manager
PRODUCER: Creative Displays Inc.

The objective was to promote the products in a selling area that would save the retailer from giving up counter space during a peak selling season. The four shelves hold a variety of products, without looking bulky or cluttered. Bronze OMA 1983.

ADVERTISER: Bonne Bell
Rod Williams, Executive VP, Marketing & Advertising
Joseph Sunseri, VP
PRODUCER: Displayco Midwest Inc.

The two-tiered tray by itself is an effective counter display, but by mounting it on the tapered pedestal, locked in by tabs die-cut from the lower tray, it becomes a floorstand. Bronze OMA 1983.

ADVERTISER: Oil of Olay, Richardson-Vicks Inc.
Ed Zarucha, Director of Merchandising Services
PRODUCER: Altwell Inc.

This handsome unit is hinged, so it can be shipped flat. To install, the riser is lifted up and the product placed in position. A sampling bottle fits in a well in the base tray. Lugs permit a special riser to be added for special promotions. Bronze OMA 1983.

ADVERTISER: Chattem Inc.
Ron Williams, Materials Control Manager
Nancy McClurd, Marketing Manager/Quencher
PRODUCER: Trans World Manufacturing Corp.

This handy salesman's kit makes a dramatic presentation, in an easy-to-carry case. It holds all three lines of lipgloss, lipstick and nail enamel, to show off the full color line and the packaging of each. Bronze OMA 1983.

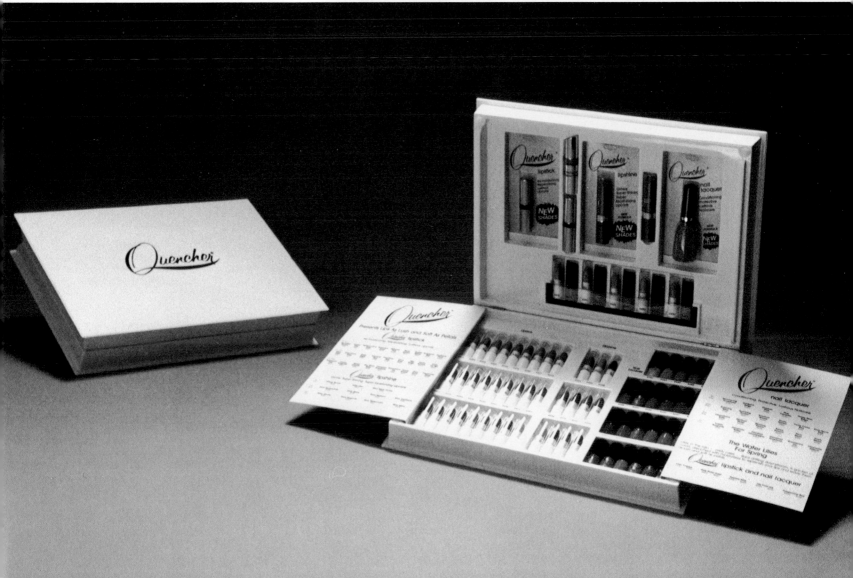

ADVERTISER: Revlon Inc.
Carmine Parisi, Display Manager
PRODUCER: Trans World Manufacturing Corp.

An enlarged working model of the product is the center of this display, which is enhanced by the intriguing *S* of the heat-bent plexiglass. Bronze OMA 1983.

ADVERTISER: Max Factor & Company
Dawn Templeton
PRODUCER: Gorrie Advertising Services
Harry Milanowski, Designer

The pristine whiteness of this simple counter display formed an excellent background for the delicate colors of the products, and gave a feeling of its clinical approach.

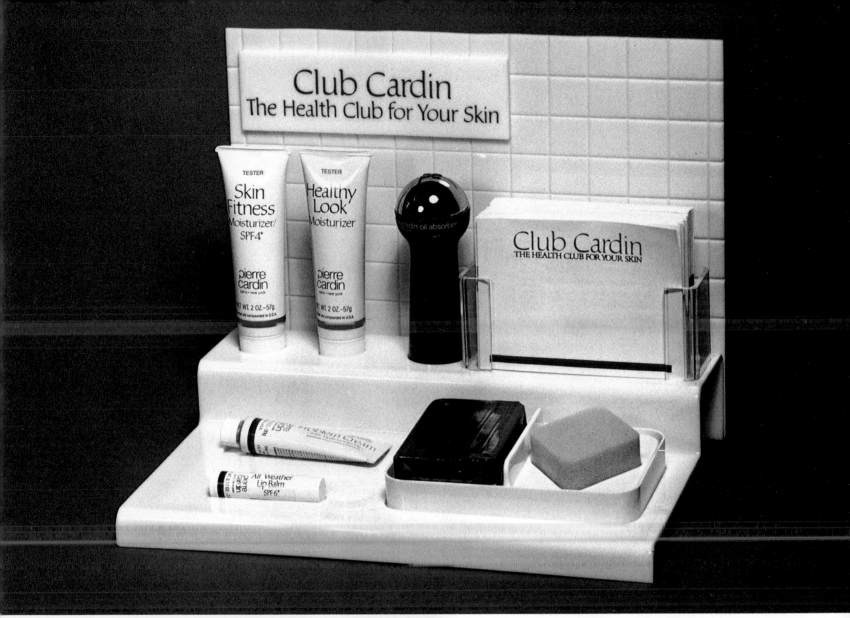

The name of the product is subtly supported by the tile-like background of this counter merchandiser.

Visual interest was added to this counter merchandiser by the angled shade chart which covered the base of the display. The prominent logo and the color illustration, reflecting the current advertising theme, focused attention on the colorful product.

ADVERTISER: G.D. Searle & Co. of Canada
Les Ashcroft
PRODUCER: Gorrie Advertising Services

Using four color lithography, this in-store promotion kit stressed
the relationship of the product to fresh fruit juices. It included price
rail inserts, headers for stacked cases, a hanging mobile, and a
window or backwall streamer.

ADVERTISER: Hudson Vitamins
James Stoddard
PRODUCER: Marketing Methods Inc.

This sturdy floor stand holds 100 pounds of vitamins, in an
organized manner, with many consumer educational messages to
simplify self-selection.

ADVERTISER: La Cross, Del Laboratories Inc.
Bill McMenemy, Group VP, Marketing
PRODUCER: Dauman Displays Inc.
Sid Dauman, Designer

This compact floor display earned prime location, even in crowded stores, and got the product line off the back wall. It can, also be removed from the base and used as a counter display. Bronze OMA 1983.

ADVERTISER: The Gillette Company
Frank Larson, Design Manager
Joe Hubblard, Project Engineer
PRODUCER: Displayco East

The pedestal carries the name of the product, while the two shelves hold more than 100 bottles of the brand. Bronze OMA 1983.

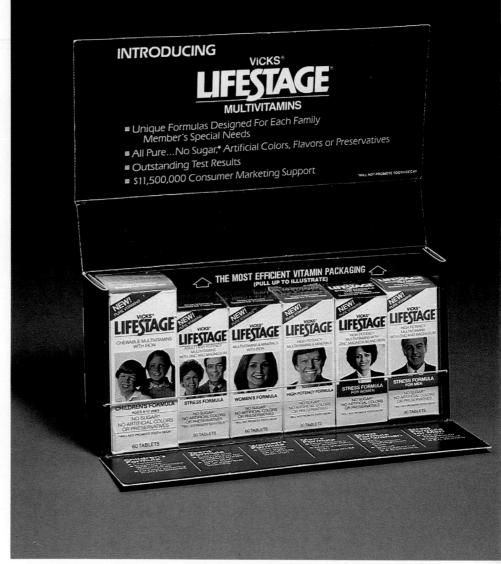

ADVERTISER: Vicks Health Care Div. Richardson-Vicks Inc.
Ed Zarucha, Director of Merchandising Services
PRODUCER: Altwell Inc.

This kit was designed to offer the sales force an attractive, effective and exciting display to introduce a new line of products. Bronze OMA 1983.

ADVERTISER: Rexall Drug Co.
Lee Fleischer, VP Marketing
PRODUCER: Displayco Midwest

This floor stand uses the header to call attention to a sweepstakes, while the colorful dangling Pac-Man characters attract attention. The two types of products are differentiated by being loaded in bi-level trays. Bronze OMA 1983.

ADVERTISER: Vita-fresh Vitamin Co.
Tom Markel, Marketing Manager
Helene Wilson, Purchasing Manager
PRODUCER: Continental Graphics
Colin Bedding, Design Director

With a line of vitamins packaged for specialized sports activities, the client wanted a unit that would illustrate its wide variety. Each tray has its distinctive color, matching the cans of product it holds. The center panel explains the nature of each vitamin type. Silver OMA 1983.

ADVERTISER: A. H. Robins Company
Robert A. Higsett, Director of Promotional Services
Gary L. James, Group Manager, Health Care Products
PRODUCER: Henschel-Steinau Inc.

This versatile display can have a variety of conformations. The recessed supports offer a greater degree of openness. The shelves can be spaced either 8- or 10-inches apart, and the header steals light from any overhead fixture. Bronze OMA 1983.

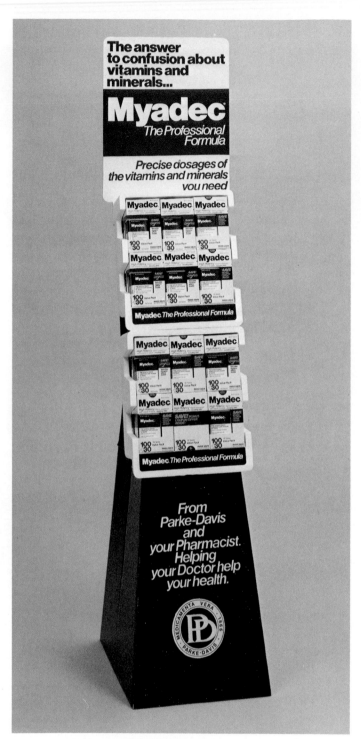

ADVERTISER: Parke-Davis, div. of Warner-Lambert
Larry Haverkost, Senior Product Manager
J. J. Fielding Jr., Trade Promotion Manager
PRODUCER: Henschel-Steinau Inc.

With only four sections, this display is easy to set up, and holds a lot of product in a little space. Bronze OMA 1983.

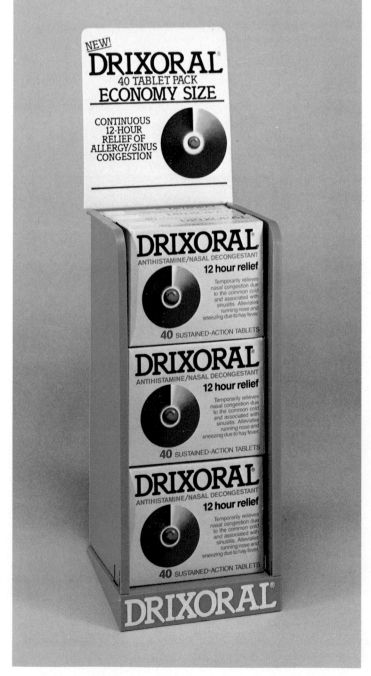

ADVERTISER: Drixoral, Schering-Plough Corp.
Joseph Trahan, Trade Marketing Manager
Howard Schwartz, Senior Product Manager
PRODUCER: Henschel-Steinau Inc.

This counter unit takes up only a three-inch space on the counter, with a bright riser card. It ships flat, saving space and cost, but can be snapped together in only 10 seconds. Bronze OMA 1983.

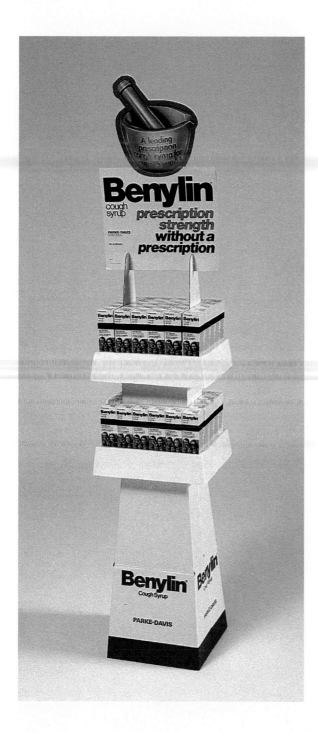

ADVERTISER: Benylin, Parke-Davis, div. of Warner Lambert
PRODUCER: Thomson-Leeds Co. Inc.

To help introduce a drug that was moving from prescription to over-the-counter sales, this two tier display was developed. Its white background and styrofoam trays called attention to the product. The trays eliminate costly packing materials, and can be used separately for counter use. A related piece was developed for very tight space conditions. Vacuum-formed in colored plastic, with an adhesive back, it can be mounted on any flat surface.

ADVERTISER: Cortaid, The Upjohn Company
Walter Ruemer, Merchandising Services Manager
PRODUCER: Henschel-Steinau Inc.

This floor stand, holding six dozen pieces, received pre-season exposure because of the coupons attached to the riser. It requires only one square foot of floor space, and because the product is packed in inner trays, it is easy to maintain. Prominent position is given to the descriptions of each of the four types of product, to make self-selection simple. Silver OMA 1983.

ADVERTISER: The Procter & Gamble Co.
John Reece, Art Director
Ruth Schwarberg, Display Material Coordinator
PRODUCER: Henschel-Steinau Inc.

The spiral arrangement of the trays, under a snowflaked, four-sided header, makes this an attractive unit. A variety of products can be displayed. The injection molded base protects the display during floor mopping. Bronze OMA 1983.

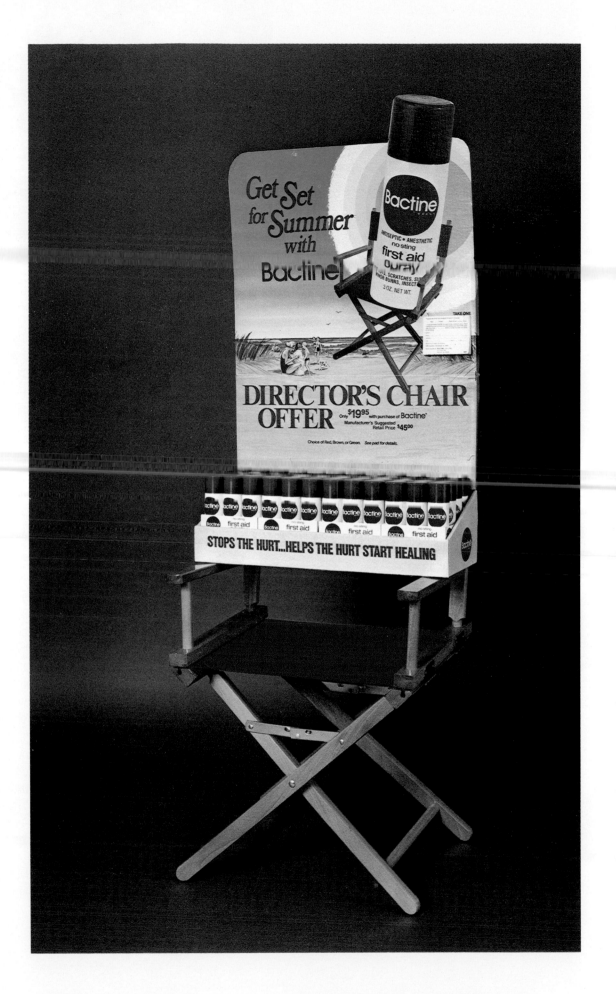

ADVERTISER: Bactine, Miles Laboratories
Dave Tingwald, Director of Sales Promotion
PRODUCER: Great Northern Corp.

Designed for a summer premium offer, this display uses an actual sample of the premium as its base, while the colorful header tells the story of the product and the promotion. Bronze OMA 1983.

POP POP POP POP POP
POP POP POP POP POP
POP POP POP POP POP
POP POP POP POP POP
POP POP POP POP POP
POP POP POP POP POP
POP POP POP POP POP
POP POP POP POP POP
POP POP POP POP

2

Foods and Paper Goods

Those executives who handle products that are sold in supermarkets will tell you that they are operating in one of the most competitive areas of all. And even a superficial observation of a supermarket in action will begin to persuade you that they are speaking the truth. The competition for shelf space, the competition for display space, and even the competition for the customer's attention, is rugged, and the designer of point-of-purchase material for this industry must work within this atmosphere, feeling the hot breath of the rival product upon the back of his neck.

Take a look at some of the figures. The average supermarket has room for some 5,000 items, considering each product, each brand, each size a separate item. While this seems like a large number, there are perhaps two or three times as many items on the market whose producers would like to have some of the available shelf space. Each item is fighting for its foot (or more, if possible) of shelf space. Since the margin on the sale of the products is very small (about 2 percent of gross), volume is important.

There is no question but that a point-of-purchase display increases the total sales of the product thus advertised. Study after study by the Point-of-Purchase Advertising Institute has demonstrated this. Giving any product a place of honor will encourage its purchase. The very fact that the product is on display will generate the initial impulse to purchase. The presence of a special display factor—light, motion—or a special promotional factor—a premium offer, a price rebate—will increase sales even further, but the initial impulse seems to be generated by the display itself.

For that reason, every product brand manager would like to get his displays used, as frequently as possible, staying up as long as possible, in as prominent a position as possible. But obviously one cannot satisfy everybody's demands. Someone must make a choice, and depending on the corporate structure and assignment of responsibility, that someone is the chain's buying office and/or the individual store manager. Thus every product manager who wishes to get support for his promotion must get over two hurdles. He must first get approval of headquarters, and then he must sell the promotion to the store itself. To do this successfully, he must take into consideration the specific objectives of the supermarket chain and its individual stores.

Raising the volume of a particular brand's sales is the objective of that brand's management, but store management is not usually concerned with the fate of any specific brand. Its objective, on the other hand, is the total profitability of the store. Brand-switching brings few benefits to supermarket management.

This thought is worth exploring a bit more. As an example, consider the market for cans of ground coffee, a highly competitive product. There are always several shelves devoted to the product, with a number of brands, many of them strongly supported by advertising. But the family that uses ground coffee uses it at a fairly steady rate, and does not usually purchase more than it needs. Since the margin on a can of coffee generally does not vary significantly with brand, a display that persuades a user of Brand A to switch to Brand B does nothing for the store's bottom line.

But if Brand B, for the duration of the promotion, offers the store a greater than usual profit, that might warrant an effort in support of Brand B, including the installation of a p.o.p. display. Or if the promotion and display encouraged the purchase of three-pound cans, instead of one-pound cans, this would bring in more cash now and would preempt the purchase of that product elsewhere. The use of an actual sample of a premium being offered tends to increase the placement of a display, since at the end of the promotion, the store manager has the item, perhaps to use as an in-store incentive, or perhaps personally.

The fact is that there are more p.o.p. displays offered to store managers than

they can possibly use. The challenge is to design a display that will meet the needs and interests of the person who makes the decision, while not neglecting the interests of the advertiser, the manufacturer of the product being promoted. And there must be valid reasons why the use of this display will help the store's bottom line. Does the display carry a special price which will increase the store's margin? Is it backed with national advertising which will create a demand and bring in customers looking for this brand? Is it offering a premium which will cause impulse or additional purchases of the product? Does the display encourage tie-in sales which increase the sales of a related item, normally a slow-moving one? Does it perform a housekeeping function within the store that will result in lower costs? Does it encourage the movement of multiple packages or large packages, and thus preempt the future market? You will find that the most successful point-of-purchase displays include at least one of these factors, and their designs stress those points.

ADVERTISER: E.J. Brach & Sons
Joseph DeAngelis
PRODUCER: AMD Industries

This permanent display has a very contemporary, clean, crisp look, with automatic stock rotation. It accommodates 12 bins for variety. OMA Best of Class.

ADVERTISER: KitKat, Hershey Foods Corp.
Doug Hoffman, Coordinator, Merchandising Development
Sam Banacci, Manager, Package Development
PRODUCER: Altwell Inc.

Immediate brand identification is achieved with this unit, through the large logos on the sides, and the six candy bars placed face up. The riser explains the sweepstakes and holds a pad of entry blanks. Bronze OMA 1983.

ADVERTISER: Ethel M. Candy
Joan Harper, Sales & Marketing
PRODUCER: Creative Displays Inc.

An elegant counter display that lets the luxurious packaging create the main interest.

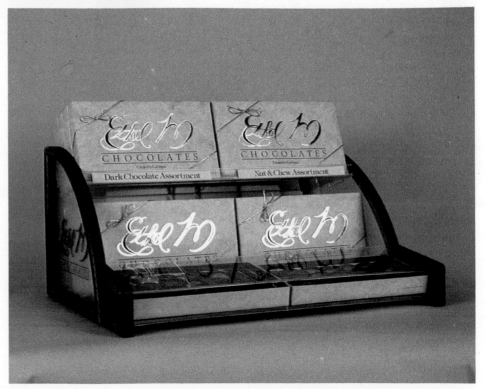

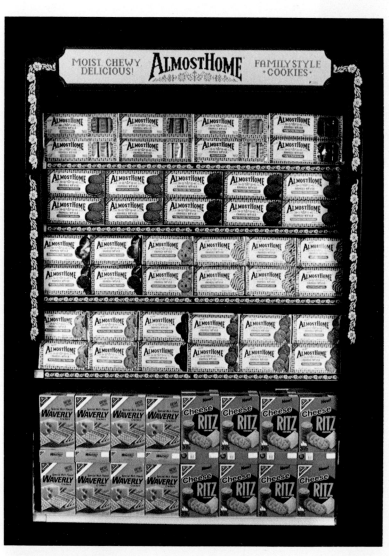

ADVERTISER: E.J. Brach & Sons
Earl Bromstedt, Natl. Merchandising Manager
PRODUCER: Wiremasters Inc.
J. M. Scriba Jr. Designer

Each of the three wire trays can hold as much as 120 pounds, yet can turn easily because of its ball thrust bearings. The loaded unit is mounted on a swivel caster which make it easy to move the unit for promotional advantage. The basket nest is for easy shipping and storage.

ADVERTISER: Almost Home, Nabisco Brands Inc.
J. M. Enock, VP, Marketing, Biscuit Group
S. A. Fordham, Marketing Manager, Biscuit Group
PRODUCER: Deijon Inc.
Vince Gambello, Designer

Picking up its design motif from the package, these simple strips that attach to existing shelving segment this cookie line from other products in the aisle. Bronze OMA 1983.

ADVERTISER: Tobler-Suchard USA Ltd.
Joseph Dattoli, Regional Sales Director
PRODUCER: Melrose Displays Inc.
Richard T. Cohen and Joseph Dattoli, Designers

Designed for gourmet food stores, this display leaves no doubt in the customer's mind of the Swiss origin of the candy. Five dump shelves and 28 compartments permit a full assortment of the product. Bronze OMA 1983.

ADVERTISER: Keebler Co.
Thomas Drake, Product Manager
Roy Koeckritz, Dir. of Merchandising, Consumer Services
PRODUCER: Designs by George Inc.

Keebler intended to increase store distribution bases and offer the convenience stores a product line developed exclusively for them. The welded wire floorstand holds the entire line, with easy loading and access for impulse sales. Gold OMA 1983.

ADVERTISER: Frito-Lay Inc.
Carl Barnhill, Merchandising Manager
Vern Lee, Sales Training Manager
PRODUCER: Mead Merchandising

Frito-Lay wished to gain incremental shelf space apart from the primary snack section. This attractive unit, with ample stacking and storage space, can vary in configuration to serve as an aisle end or as an island. The decorative roof piece can be centered over the unit, regardless of what size is used. Bronze OMA 1983.

ADVERTISER: Guy's Foods, Borden Inc.
Rich Nestman, Director of Sales Promotion
PRODUCER: Great Northern Corp.

Designed to gain additional off-shelf space for a specialty product, the unit had to have the ability to be assembled and taken down several times over an extended period. Metal rods glued into the shelf fronts prevent damage in assembly and disassembly. Bronze OMA 1983.

ADVERTISER: Grandma's, Frito-Lay Inc.
Ed Resh, Creative Services Manager
PRODUCER: Weyerhaeuser Co.

The design of this header, planned to sit on cut cases of cookies, uses a blow-up of characters from the product's TV advertising.

ADVERTISER: Piper Hill, Goodhost Foods Ltd.
Lisa Slater, President
Charlie Mattina, National Brand Manager
PRODUCER: CDA Industries Inc.

Ten clear bins, with plexiglass front, make the coffee beans visible. The customer can make his selection, withdrawing beans from the bottom while refills go into the top, thus assuring product turnover. Bronze OMA 1983.

ADVERTISER: Hefty, div. of Mobil Chemical Co.
PRODUCER: Thomson-Leeds Co. Inc.

Paper plates are bulky and during the busy season, it is hard to keep enough stock in a display. This center aisle merchandiser offers great visibility, easy access, and simple reloading from the top.

ADVERTISER: Kimberly Clark Corp.
Les Smith, Manager Client Services/Communication Services
PRODUCER: Acorn Display

This dealer kit is designed to dramatize the promotion that Kleenex belongs everywhere in the house. The two-story dollhouse, corrugated, shows Kleenex in use in every room. After the presentation, the unit is left with the dealer, and may be used by him as a display. Gold OMA 1983.

ADVERTISER: Quik, The Nestle Co.
PRODUCER: Thomson-Leeds Co. Inc.

A special Thanksgiving promotion was designed to offer customers a free fun booklet and a chance to win a turkey. The cut-case display featured the Quik bunny, tying in with the national advertising campaign.

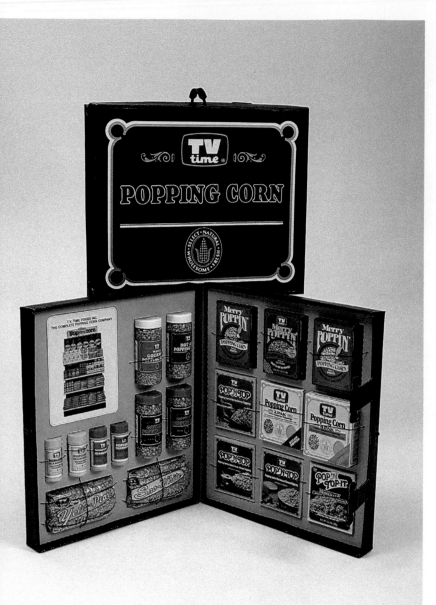

ADVERTISER: TV Time Popcorn, McCormick & Co.
PRODUCER: Thomson-Leeds Co. Inc.

An inexpensive corrugated case, measuring only 1½ by 1¾ ft. was used to help salesmen introduce a new product line to prospective retail accounts. Actual samples of each item in the line were easily presented to the buyer.

ADVERTISER: Carnation
Jim Richards, Director of Graphic Printing
PRODUCER: Continental Graphics

The motion of the sunburst behind the replica of the sack grabbed attention to this pole display wherever it was placed.

ADVERTISER: The Kellogg Company
PRODUCER: Great Northern Corporation

This tropical hut made a spectacular header for a mass display of products calling attention to a special Safari promotion. At the option of the store, it could be used as a special prize at that store.

ADVERTISER: Durkee Famous Foods
A. M. Kazal, Product Manager
Michael E. Diskin, Product Manager
PRODUCER: Merchandising Display Corp.

Featuring the "Best of the Seasons" Sweepstakes, this free-standing unit included a mixture of five major pre-packs. Included with the display were shelf-talkers, price cards and case cards designed to encourage shoppers to seek out the display. Bronze OMA 1983.

ADVERTISER: Top Secret, Ralston Purina
Henry Brinkley, Purchasing Agent
PRODUCER: E. and E. Specialties
Nelson Orwig, Designer

An inexpensive corrugated pre-pack, with a cut-away base, has earned good locations for an unglamorous product.

ADVERTISER: L&M, Liggett & Myers Tobacco Co. Inc.
Richard D. Haynes Jr., Supervisor, Graphic Services
PRODUCER: The Hennegan Company

To establish brand recognition of a new product, a dispenser shaped like a cigarette pack is an attention-getter. The two-for-one offer is stated prominently. Bronze OMA 1983.

ADVERTISER: Camel, R.J. Reynolds Tobacco Co.
Walt Whiteman, Group Merchandising Manager
PRODUCER: Thomas A. Schutz Co.

Trays and posts are designed to snap together in many different configurations, to make maximum use of available space. There is even a fixture that will clamp to any vertical or horizontal bar, tube, or pegboard. Silver OMA 1983.

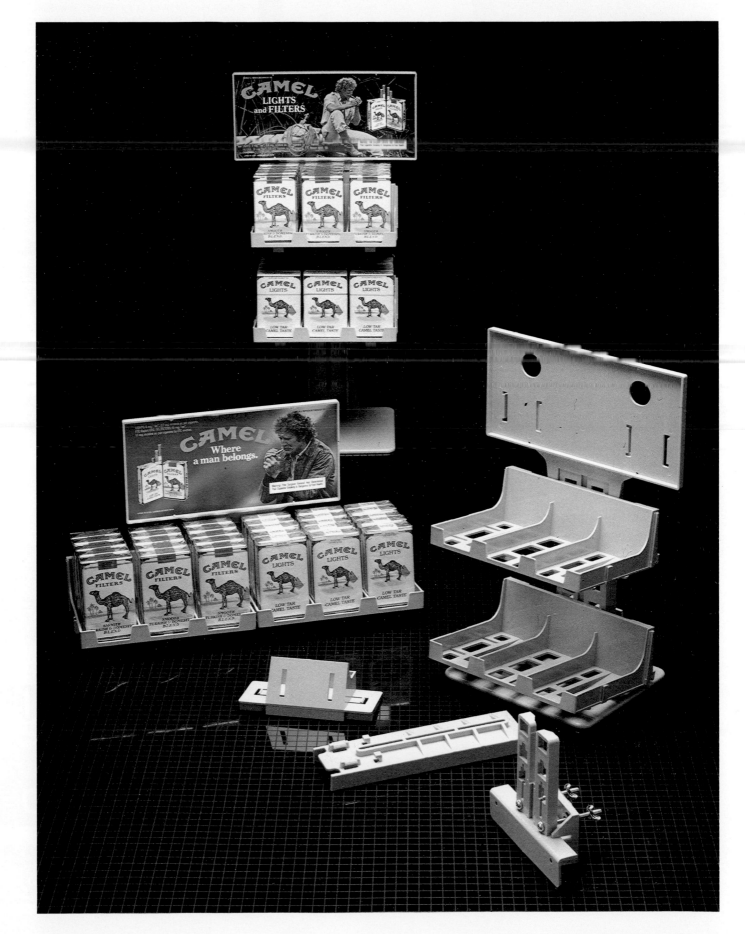

ADVERTISER: Camel, R.J. Reynolds Tobacco Co.
K. B. Hedrick, Group Manager, P-O-S Advertising Development
Barbara Alford, Senior Buyer
PRODUCER: DCI Marketing

Developed for use in all U.S. markets, this display commands attention while not taking up any valuable counter space. It can be customized with the store's logo. The numerals are stored within the sign by unclipping one of the endcaps. Bronze OMA 1983.

ADVERTISER: Camel, R.J. Reynolds Tobacco Co.
K. B. Hedrick, Group Manager, P-O-S Advertising Development
Barbara Alford, Senior Buyer
PRODUCER: H. King & Associates Ltd.

Designed to sit on top of a cigarette vending machine, this unit is especially valuable to remind buyers of a brand for which no room can be found in the machine. Its slanted base keeps patrons from placing (and spilling) beverage cups or cans on the vending machine. The illuminated version can also be used as a night light. Bronze OMA 1983.

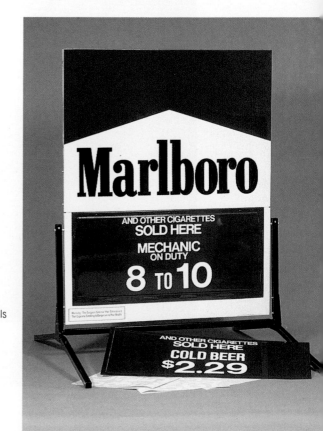

ADVERTISER: Marlboro, Philip Morris USA
William Cutler, Director, Merchandising Materials
Phyllis Kornbluth, Supervisor, Merchandising Materials
PRODUCER: Stout Industries Inc.

Here is a curb stand that offers a flexible message area. Vinyl cut-out letters, guaranteed to last two years, can be mounted easily, and removed when desired. Bronze OMA 1983.

This digital clock is the largest now available, and tells the month and day as well as the time. Store logos or local messages can be included between the ad and the clock. Silver OMA 1983.

One effective wall piece includes a digital clock, changeable product and price panels, and room for a store logo. Bronze OMA 1983.

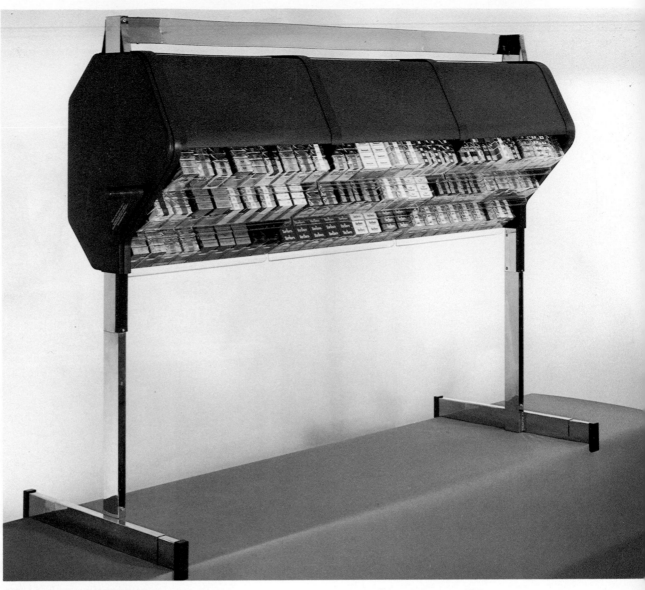

ADVERTISER: Philip Morris USA
William Cutler, Director of Merchandising Materials
William Cook, Manager of Merchandising Materials
PRODUCER: Henschel-Steinau Inc.

Here is an attractive, contemporary, merchandising vehicle that uses vacant air space above front counters. It holds more than 1,000 packs of cigarettes which are gravity fed. The side facing the customer holds replacable graphic panels. The unit can be hung from the ceiling as well as using the counter stand shown here. Bronze OMA 1983.

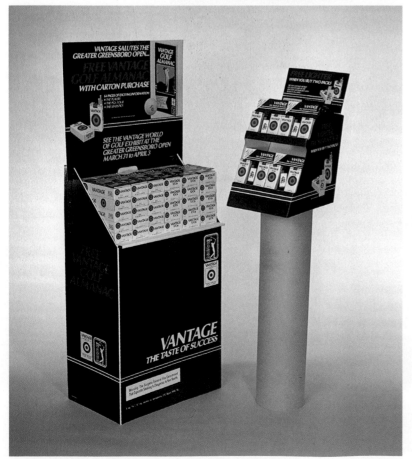

ADVERTISER: Vantage, R.J. Reynolds Tobacco Co.
Brenda Smelcer, Purchasing Coordinator
PRODUCER: Glover Advertising Inc.

These two units help associate the brand with professional golf and the local tournament, with the latter mentioned on the changeable header. Bronze OMA 1983.

ADVERTISER: Red Man, The Pinkerton Tobacco Co.
Marshall May, Vice President
David Stiele, Senior Product Manager
PRODUCER: Advertising Display Co.

This successful promotion called attention to the cap offer, and made it easy to pick up pouches of the product. Cartons of pouches were held in the base. Since no markings appear on the bin, it can be used for later promotions by changing the riser. Bronze OMA 1983.

ADVERTISER: Work Horse, R.J. Reynolds Tobacco Co.
Norton Willis
PRODUCER: Southern Corrugated Box Co.
Rick Schum, Designer

Picking up a theme from television and printed advertising, this standing display encourages impulse purchases.

POPPOPPOPPOP
POPPOPPOPPOP
POPPOPPOPPOP
POPPOPPOPPOP
POPPOPPOPPOP
POPPOPPOPPOP
POPPOPPOPPOP
POPPOPPOPPOP

3

Household Goods

One thinks of household goods as traditional, long-lasting items, purchased only after serious consideration—and certainly these terms apply to much of the category. The purchase of a refrigerator or a freezer, or a bedroom suite or a living-room sofa, is not usually an impulsive action, and the point-of-purchase advertising that is developed for these products reflects this attitude. When a large outlay of personal funds is under consideration, the consumer looks for a lot of input before making the purchase. He talks to his peers, to other owners of the contemplated item; he reads consumer magazines and manufacturers' brochures.

With products in this category, point-of-purchase advertising is the silent salesperson who informs the potential consumer of product benefits. It replaces the often absent salesperson, and sometimes it is considered a more reliable source of information—a direct message from the manufacturer, undistorted by the self-imposed and suspiciously viewed pressure of the salesperson. The displays for this category must not only help create awareness, presence, and excitement, but

present information as well. Using the simultaneous presence of consumer, cash, and product, the display must help the motion towards a rational decision to buy—on the spot.

But the next few pages obviously give a different impression. In addition to displays designed to support those high level, rationally purchased articles, this chapter also contains displays that are designed to produce impulse purchases, more akin to the supermarket psychology than what would be expected from major purchase areas. These fall into two mercurial segments of the broad household-goods market: small appliances and home entertainment products.

Small appliances may be a peculiarly American phenomenon. From the very beginning of our history we seem to have been fascinated by gadgets. Our colonial homes, reconstructed at places like Stur-

bridge or Williamsburg, seem to be filled with ingenious mechanical devices designed to do specialized jobs like peeling apples, pitting cherries, or toasting bread at the fireplace. We have carried on this tradition with electric and electronic gadgets of today, gadgets which are not usually necessities and therefore must be sold. These must be presented in an intriguing way, first to catch the shopper's fancy, then to make him or her feel the necessity of possessing this item, and finally to move the consumer to make the purchase. This is a function well within the power of point-of-purchase advertising, and the medium has come through.

The sub-category of home entertainment is itself a broad one. It includes, of course, such major articles as color television sets and stereo sound systems—hardly impulsive purchases. On the other hand, it also encompasses home computer systems, which need support in the marketplace in an educational direction, and this kind of promotional material is demonstrated in this section of the book.

Finally, we enter the domain of computer software. Computer games, whether on disk or cartridge, are essentially impulse items. They are inexpensive objects (at least in the world of computer owners) which have no purpose but to provide entertainment, and as such are acquired for the sheer pleasure of satisfying an impulse. Point-of-purchase materials must help to create awareness, presence, and excitement. Producers of games must be ready to move quickly in recognizing the appeal of a new product, in supporting it when there is evidence of the beginning of a fad, and in continually keeping the product on the move and in the public eye. The environment for this kind of promotion is one in which space is at a premium, and in which every possibility for display must be utilized.

ADVERTISER: Duracell, Div. of P.R. Mallory
PRODUCER: Thompson-Leeds Co. Inc.

To serve as a constant reminder on buyers' desks, a stock paper clip holder was modified to take on the appearance of a dry cell. A wrapping of a printed Mylar label, laminated for protection, achieves the transformation.

ADVERTISER: Pioneer Electronics (USA) Inc.
Chris Byrne, VP, Home Audio Marketing
PRODUCER: DCI Marketing Inc.

Pioneer required a display that would hold a complete audio system, including tuner, amplifier, sound processor, cassette recorder, turntable, and speakers, in a minimal floor space. This merchandiser, with all wiring concealed, does the job and blends with all types of store decor.

ADVERTISER: Panasonic
PRODUCER: Ledan Inc.

This three-dimensional hand, holding a working model of the new product, was bound to call attention to this new calculator.

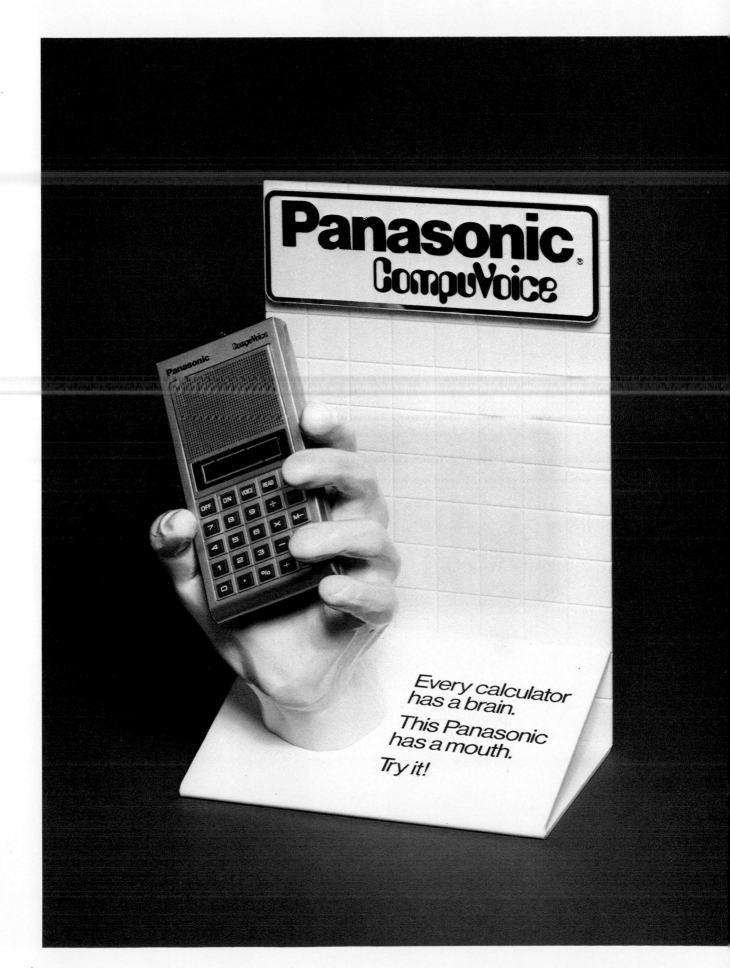

ADVERTISER: Sony of Canada
Doug Willox
PRODUCER: Gorrie Advertising Services
Paul Whittington, Designer

This corrugated dump bin attracted attention with its large logo and its bright colors on the base. It could be used for many products within the Sony line.

ADVERTISER: The Counselor Co. Newell Companies
PRODUCER: Weyerhaeuser Company

This pedestal scale was difficult to display in a knock-down form, and yet it could be shipped and stored economically only if unassembled. This ingenious package allowed the unit to be displayed in its own shipping carton. Bronze OMA 1983.

ADVERTISER: Nikko/Sansui
PRODUCER: Ridan Displays
John Gross

This identification sign can either be mounted on the wall, or placed on a counter.

ADVERTISER: Eveready Batteries, Union Carbide
George Ghesquiere
PRODUCER: AMD Industries Inc.
Raymond Baluk, Designer

The modular units in this system come in two-foot, three-foot and four-foot sizes, and can be used for in-line, island, or end-cap displays. Made of tin plate sheet metal and high-gloss finished hardboard, these rigid displays can support the substantial weight of a full complement of batteries and lighting products.

ADVERTISER: Seiko, Kaman Music Distributors
Gabe Ireland, VP, Marketing
PRODUCER: Displayco East
Dennis Claussen, Designer

A selection of timers and small tuning devices were brought by this sleek unit from the remote shelves behind the counter within reach of customers. The sleek unit is easily moved to a desirable location.

ADVERTISER: Sony of Canada
Doug Willox
PRODUCER: Gorrie Advertising Services
Harry Milowicz, Designer

This in-store program was designed to complement the theme that had been used in print and video advertising.

GORRIE ADVERTISING SERVICES

ADVERTISER: Sony of Canada
Doug Willox
PRODUCER: Gorrie Advertising Services
Paul Whittington, Designer

This full-line counter display permitted any of the products to be tested, but they are unobtrusively locked in position to thwart pilferage

ADVERTISER: Sears, Roebuck and Company
Lee Schwartz, National Display Manager
PRODUCER: Frank Mayer and Associates Inc.

This counter system, with four pods, permits consumers to see what they are shopping for, to compare features and help them make up their minds without the assistance of a salesman. The four-part unit can sit on a shelf with boxed stock on the lower shelves for convenient selection. Bronze OMA 1983.

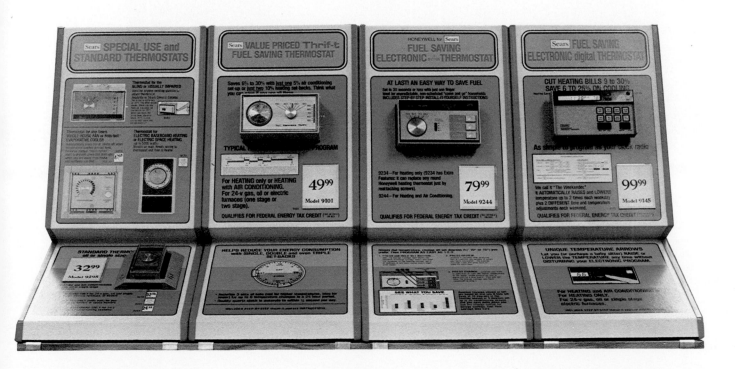

Advertiser: General Electric Co.
Stu Dean, Manager, Dishwasher Marketing
Tom Butler, Merchandising Specialist

Producer: Harbor Industries Inc.

Two new dishwashers, top of the line, needed separation from the others being offered. This special floor display not only showed how the units would look when installed, but contained the electronic controls to permit prospects to touch the buttons. Electronic sound and LED readout make the unit reponsive. Bronze OMA.

ADVERTISER: Decart
Anka Kriser, President
PRODUCER: Creative Displays Inc.

This flower stall, designed for high traffic areas in department stores, uses its wheels to suggest the romantic flower peddler.

ADVERTISER: EKCO
Bob Ciucci
PRODUCER: Creative Displays Inc.

This distinctive selling center uses its natural wood finish to set off the metal kitchen tools.

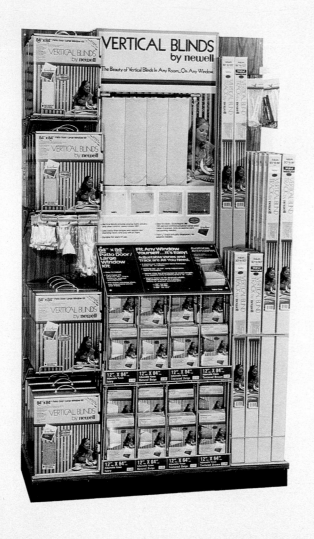

ADVERTISER: Newell Companies Inc.
PRODUCER: Thomson-Leeds Co. Inc.

A one-stop buying and information center, this unit displays the product forcefully, gives information needed for a buying decision, and holds adequate inventory. The display can be set up by one person in less than 20 minutes, and using a special fastener, can be assembled completely from the front. In 1983, it received the Gold Drummer award from *Building Supply News*.

ADVERTISER: Wilton Enterprises
            Joseph DeAngelis
PRODUCER: AMD Industries Inc.
            Raymond Baluk, Designer

This compact unit, 47 in. wide, 12 in. deep, and 21 in. high, fits on the top shelf of an existing display or a counter top. It organizes and improves product presentation to prompt add-on sales.

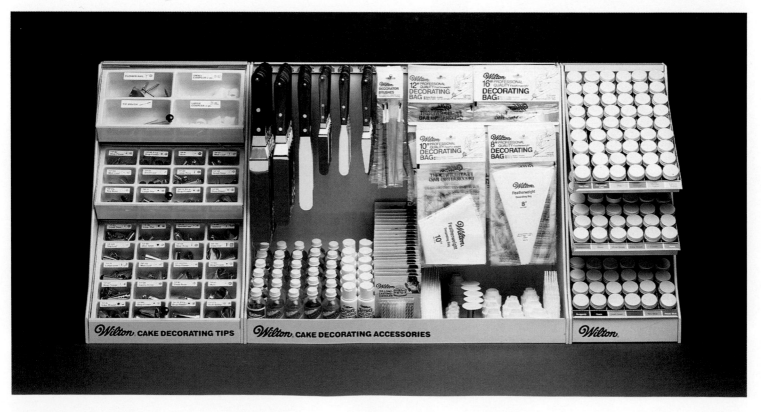

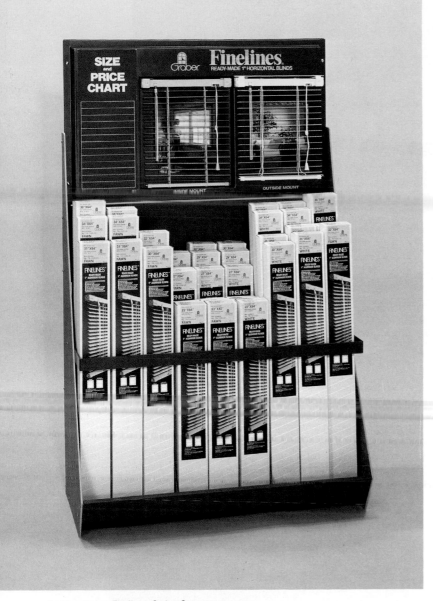

ADVERTISER: Finelines, Graber Company
Terry Putty, Merchandising Manager
PRODUCER: AMD Industries Inc.
Frank Shade, Designer

A complete blind department is contained in a unit occupying only three linear feet. Two miniature blinds demonstrate both mounting and operating characteristics, while the base holds three dozen packages.

ADVERTISER: Levolor Lorentzen Inc.
William A. Keyser, Senior VP
Harold Reiss, Marketing Director
PRODUCER: The Howard/Marlboro Group
Howard Nathan, Designer

This unit was designed to establish distribution through outlets not reached by the client, like mass merchandisers, discount stores, home improvement centers, etc. The self standing display contained a demonstration unit, a brochure holder, and room for price information, plus a selection of inventory. Bronze OMA 1983.

ADVERTISER: Braun Canada
Mike Meehan
PRODUCER: Gorrie Advertising Services
Paul Whittington, Designer

The white plastic of this display matches the color of the
equipment, and the unit allows all the accessories to be displayed.

ADVERTISER: Republic Molding
Bill Wolf, VP, Marketing
Tom Kemp, Western Sales Manager
PRODUCER: Willamette Industries
Bennie Nelson, Designer

This continuity promotion features 12 items. The self-standing
display permitted each item to be put forward during its special
week, allowed the customer to see all 12 items, and had room to
store the product line. Bronze OMA 1983.

ADVERTISER: Seiko/Picco Division
Dick Fortunato
PRODUCER: Einson Freeman
Stan Levine, Designer

A package which holds the product as if it were floating in the air serves as an attractive display.

ADVERTISER: Bissell Inc.
Jack Hughes, General Sales Manager
Charles Huhn, Advertising Director
PRODUCER: Wiremasters Inc.
J. M. Scriba Jr., Designer

The wire unit ships flat and sets up quickly. It displays the cleaning unit, using the four-color graphics of the empty carton as an eye-catcher. This also keeps the packing materials convenient for when the unit is sold off the stand. Bronze OMA 1983.

Advertiser: Atari Inc.
Robert Lindsey, Director of Marketing Services
Producer: DCI Marketing

This counter unit permits an unmanned demonstration of the Atari home computer. The metal framework holds the computer and any television set securely, while the cartridge is protected by a cable security system. The mobile, with an enlarged replica of one of the most popular and familiar games, calls attention to the unit.

ADVERTISER: Pac-Man, Atari Inc.
Alice Locke
PRODUCER: Corky Chapman Associates

Special rocker arms, die-cut of Fome-Cor, give extra dimension to what is otherwise a flat display. 1st place, San Francisco Ad Club Competition, 1982.

ADVERTISER: Gravitar, Atari Coin-Op Division
George Opperman, Head, Atari Coin-Op Div., Designer
PRODUCER: Corky Chapman Associates

This mobile, made of Fome-Cor, has special debossing around the letters of the game.

Advertiser: Swordquest, Atari
Alice Locke
Kathy Wright, Designer
Producer: Corky Chapman Associates

Die-cut from Monsanto's Fome-Cor board, this complex mobile is light in weight, but retains rigidity.

Advertiser: Atari International
Chris Peck
Jan Davis, Designer
Producer: Corky Chapman Associates
Patrick O'Daniels, Designer

This counter tent card says '**new**' in 10 languages. Note the care in airbrushing so that the design matches on two side pieces.

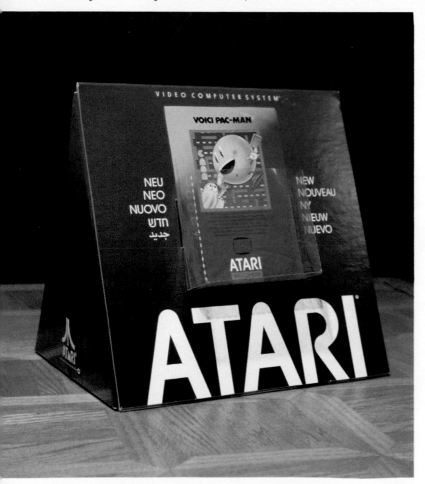

Advertiser: Centipede, Atari
Russell Brown, Designer
Producer: DCI Marketing Inc.

Complex motion was introduced without motors by the use of a spring wire for hanging. The characters simulate their action in the game itself.

ADVERTISER: Atari Inc.
Alice Locke
PRODUCER: Corky Chapman Associates

This two-sided display dispenses coupons on both faces.

ADVERTISER: E.T., Atari Inc; Atari Int.
Alice Locke
PRODUCER: Corky Chapman Associates
Jan Davis (Int.) & Jim Massey (Domestic), Designers

The coordinated displays—a mobile, a counter card, and a dump display—use elements from the motion picture. The international display (left) features a plastic pocket which permits the entire brochure to be seen.

ADVERTISER: Activision Inc.
Barbara Rose
PRODUCER: Corky Chapman Associates
Patrick O'Daniels, Designer

Utilizing four-color artwork, this die-cut countercard and poster adds impact with a die-cut head of an alligator that pops out.

ADVERTISER: Seaquest, Activision Inc.
Barbara Rose
PRODUCER: Corky Chapman Associates
Patrick O'Daniels, Designer

The interest of dimension is added with a die-cut diver mounted on the card.

ADVERTISER: Activision Inc.
Barbara Rose
PRODUCER: Corky Chapman Associates
Patrick O'Daniels, Designer

Utilizing four-color artwork, this die-cut countercard and poster adds impact with a a die-cut head of an alligator that pops out.

ADVERTISER: Enduro, Activision Inc.
Ralph Giuffre
PRODUCER: Corky Chapman Associates
Patrick O'Daniels, Designer

Starting with an ad created for a magazine campaign, the racing squares were added to bring the display to the required width.

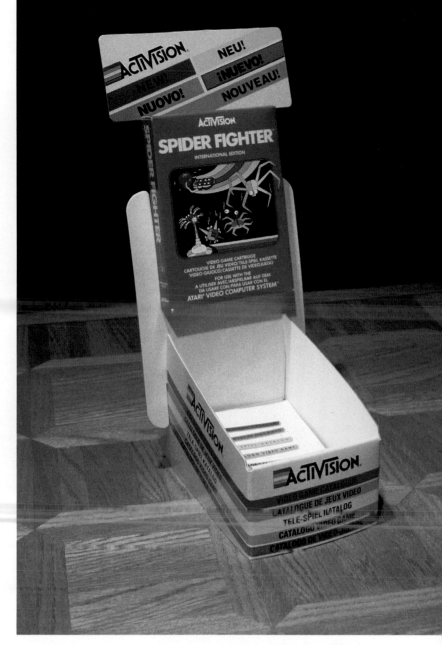

ADVERTISER: Activision Inc.
Barbara Rose
PRODUCER: Corky Chapman Associates
Patrick O'Daniels, Designer

Utilizing four-color artwork, this die-cut countercard and poster adds impact with a die-cut head of an alligator that pops out.

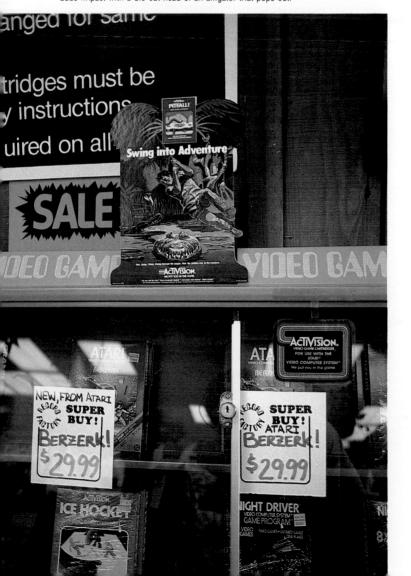

ADVERTISER: Activision International
Stuart Allardice
PRODUCER: Corky Chapman Associates
Patrick O'Daniels, Designer

Designed to dispense catalogs, this display gains interest by sliding a box from a currently active game over the header, thus extending the shelf life of the unit.

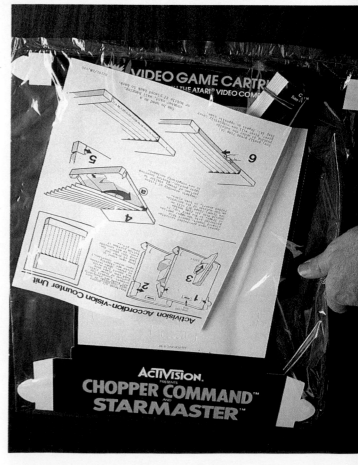

ADVERTISER: Activision Inc.
Barbara Rose
PRODUCER: Corky Chapman Associates
Patrick O'Daniels, Designer

Which of the two posters you see depends on your angle of vision. If two are mounted back to back, the unit can be hung to produce a mobile.

ADVERTISER: Activision Inc.
Barbara Rose
PRODUCER: Corky Chapman Associates
Aaron Friedman (The Display Mart), Designer

This acrylic display holds a 6×8 in. printed sheet that can be changed easily as new video games are released. An empty box slides over the top.

ADVERTISER: Atari Inc.
Robert Lindsey, Director of Marketing Services
PRODUCER: DCI Marketing Inc.

This is a center where customers are invited to try out a selection of software cartridges, while getting a real hands-on feel of the unit. Surrounding the live video screen are vignettes showing other kinds of computer activity. Bronze OMA 1983.

ADVERTISER: Atari Home Computers
Robert Lindsey, Director of Marketing Services
Tony Sparaco, Merchandise Manager

PRODUCER: The Howard/Marlboro Group

Two similar units were designed, one for hardware and one for software. The hardware unit has an interactive video disc program running continuously. The customer can use the computer to try the equipment and to work with the disc program. The software packages are kept in drawers with clear plastic fronts, through which you can see one package, locked in place to deter replacement by competitive brands. This makes it colorful and convenient for selection and inventory.

ADVERTISER: Spinnaker Software
PRODUCER: Deijon Inc.

This rotating counter display permits as many as 12 software packages to be seen in full facings. The spines are also fully visible. It was one of seven P.O.P. award winners at the Winter Consumer Electronics Show.

ADVERTISER: Sears, Roebuck and Company
Lee Schwartz, National Display Manager
PRODUCER: Frank Mayer and Associates Inc.

A touch of the button permits the customer to choose any of 45 video games, substituting for the traditional task of asking a clerk to insert a cartridge. Two boards, placed above the video screen, use changable slats to keep a best-seller list. Bronze OMA 1983.

ADVERTISER: General Electric Co.
Kathleen Goldman, Specialist, Advertising & Sales Promotion
PRODUCER: Frank Mayer and Associates Inc.

A series of related units constitute the kit that can enhance a demonstration television set. The remote control is locked into a bracket to permit its use, while discouraging theft. Bronze OMA 1983.

ADVERTISER: Generic
PRODUCER: Deijon Inc.

This display unit permits the customer to see a large number of compact discs in the minimum space, keeping the graphics fully visible, and yet preventing pilferage of the small packages. The locked base holds additional inventory.

ADVERTISER: Activision Inc.
Mark Beaumont
PRODUCER: Corky Chapman Associates
Patrick O'Daniels

The old-fashioned Santa holds the coupon box in his die-cut hand.

ADVERTISER: Hennegan Co.
Bob Ott
PRODUCER: Dyment Co.
Tom Rich, Designer

This three-dimensional life-size character brings great authenticity to the movie display.

ADVERTISER: Hennegan Co.
Bob Ott
PRODUCER: Dyment Co.
Tom Rich, Designer

Two motion pictures share this three-dimensional display, using characters and scenes from the films.

ADVERTISER: RCA Consumer Electronics
Laurence Small, Manager Retail Advertising
Rose Dress, Buyer Graphic Art
PRODUCER: DCI Marketing Inc.

A high-tech display was needed for a high-tech product. This
illuminated, formed dome with its grid graphics and the prominent
placement of the instruction booklet called attention to the product
and invited the prospect to see and try for himself.

ADVERTISER: Generic
PRODUCER: Deijon Inc.
Vincent Gambello, Designer

This patented merchandising system, made of clear, injection—molded plastic, displays more merchandise in the same amount of space, thus increasing the profit per square foot.

▶

ADVERTISER: Generic
PRODUCER: Deijon Inc.

Designed especially for the new compact discs, these plastic shelves can be placed easily on a peg-board wall, and hold the packages securely, but without obscuring their graphics.

ADVERTISER: Generic
PRODUCER: Deijon Inc.
Vincent Gambello, Designer

This patented merchandising system, made of clear, injection-molded plastic, displays more merchandise in the same amount of space, thus increasing the profit per square foot.

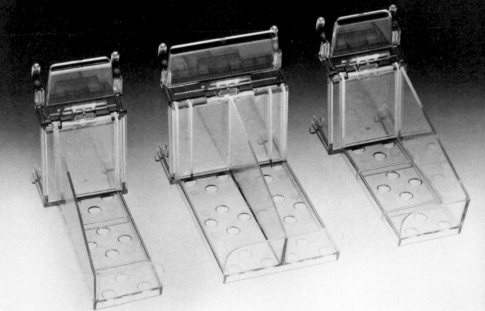

POPPOPPOPPOP
POPPOPPOPPOP
POPPOPPOPPOPPOP
POPPOPPOPPOP
POPPOPPOPPOPPOP
POPPOPPOPPOP
POPPOPPOPPOPPO
POPPOPPOPPOP
POPPOPPOPPOPPP
POPPOPPOPPO

4

Hardware/ Building Materials

There is probably no category in this book in which point-of-purchase advertising is as important in its utilitarian contribution as in its promotional one. To see why this should be true, one must look at the nature of the products included, as well as at the nature of the places in which the products are distributed.

In the first place, most of the products are unglamorous. There is nothing exciting about a nail or a screw. But to a person with a job to be done, the choice of a nail is an important—and not always simple— decision. The differences between one nail and another are slight, but important, and most customers have no basis for selection. They need help, and they must get help before they make their final selection.

On the other side of the picture, the retailer is faced with a serious problem in terms of his personnel's time. His customers come with questions that must be answered before a purchase will be made. The questions are often very de- tailed. Do I need a 1in. or a 1¼ in. screw? What tools must I have to replace a faucet washer? Which washer should I get? But answering questions takes time, and time must be paid for.

Point-of-purchase advertising can come to the rescue. Good p.o.p. helps customers find the answers to their questions. It presents the products in a logical manner, indicating clearly the differences among the items on display, and if possible,

giving criteria for selection. It also groups related items together, so that the customer's selection process is speeded up. It reduces the chances of the customer leaving without having purchased an essential item whose absence will be noted only when the job is halfway done and everything is in the maximum state of disorder. (How many of us have sweated out the job of cleaning out or replacing a messy kitchen sink trap, getting all the parts dismantled and spread on the now-greasy kitchen floor, starting to reassemble the pipes, only to find that we omitted to get a new gasket?)

Increasing the efficiency of the store staff is an immediate benefit of effective point-of-purchase. But cutting down on the time required to field customers' questions is only one of the benefits of good p.o.p. Another is the improved organization of stock. Hardware items come in families, and as is often true in families, its members tend to look alike. There are only slight differences between one kind of nut and bolt and another, and there are many sizes, styles, and materials of nuts and bolts. The differences may seem inconsequential when the line is looked at with a limited concern, but once the customer begins looking for a specific item for a specific task, those differences become crucial.

Inventory control is a tremendous problem under the circumstances, and many of the display units shown in this chapter are designed to make it easy to keep track of what is on hand and what is getting low. They are shelf organizers and even miniature departments. This means, of course, that they tend to be made of more permanent materials, of heavier construction, and have longer use than some of the temporary units more common in supermarkets.

Promotional units are not absent from hardware and building supply outlets. After all, many small appliances are sold through these channels. The reasons that motivate small-appliance purchases do not appear to vary considerably between one type of store and another. But because of the somewhat different demographics, small-appliance displays designed for hardware and building-supply outlets tend to be somewhat more educational and less promotional than those in more popular markets.

ADVERTISER: The Sherwin Williams Company
Jack Wallace, Creative Director of Merchandising and Store Planning
Chris Connor, Director of Advertising and Retail Merchandising
PRODUCER: DCI Marketing Inc.

In a single counter unit, the problem of disappearing color chips is solved. Customers may remove color chips in which they are interested, but the bottom of the stack is held permanently in place. Each section of the rack swings forward to permit access to the reserve supply. Incandescent illumination simulates home lighting conditions. Bronze OMA 1983.

ADVERTISER: Sherwin-Williams
Jack Wallace
PRODUCER: Patrick H. Joyce & Associates
Hal Nickel, Designer

Forty color strips are held in this dignified counter display, along with holders for literature, and some samples which show finish.

ADVERTISER: Colony Paints, Valspar Corp.
Michael C. Spangler
PRODUCER: Benchmarc Displays Inc.
Edwin Miller, Designer

This panel gave complete information on multi-purpose enamel coatings. Die-cut foam core chips showed standard colors and finishes; paint chips suggested the range of custom colors, and color illustrations showed the completed process.

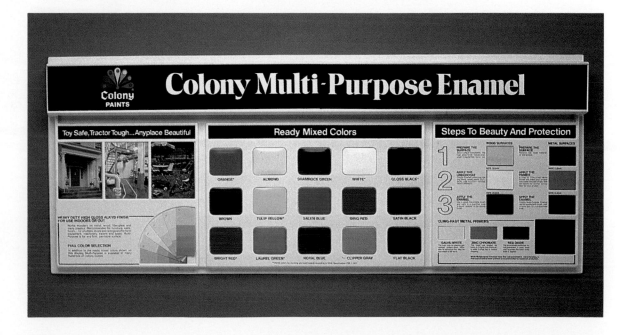

ADVERTISER: Colony Paints, Valspar Corp.
Michael C. Spangler
PRODUCER: Benchmarc Displays Inc.
Edwin Miller, Designer

These panels, which could be mounted on walls or on the tops of
gondolas, informed the consumer about the qualities of the paint.
Large paint chips show the sheen that could be achieved; smaller
chips called attention to custom colors; replicas of the cans, with
actual labels, helped customers find what they want on the shelves;
and the copy points out benefits.

ADVERTISER: Georgia-Pacific
Alan Thielemann, Director of Marketing Communications
PRODUCER: Multiplex Display Fixture Co.
George J. Buzkij, Designer

A simple rack holds an assortment of literature where customers
can browse to find those that interest them. They are easy to
remove and easy to replace.

ADVERTISER: Georgia-Pacific
Alan Thielemann, Director of Marketing Communications
PRODUCER: Multiplex Display Fixture Co.
George J. Buzkij, Designer

A large panel with full-color photos shows the product in use, along with product literature, while a full array of samples is easily reached.

ADVERTISER: Colony Paints, Valspar Corp.
Michael C. Spangler
PRODUCER: Benchmarc Displays Inc.
Edwin Miller, Designer

These panels, which could be mounted on walls or on the tops of gondolas, informed the consumer about the qualities of the paint. Large paint chips show the sheen that could be achieved; smaller chips call attention to custom colors; replicas of the cans, with actual labels, help customers find what they want on the shelves; and the copy points out benefits.

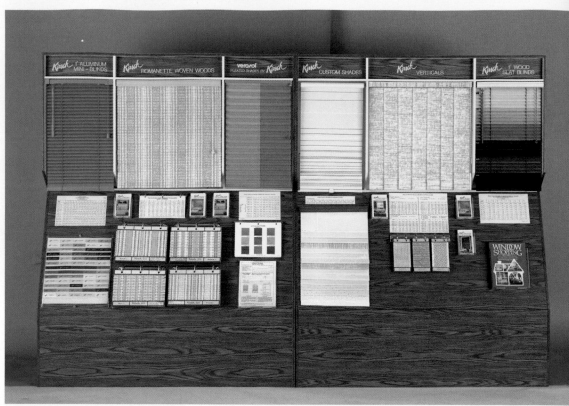

ADVERTISER: Kirsch Company
PRODUCER: Kirsch Company
Jill Armstrong, Sales Promotion Manager

This self-standing unit, consisting of six modules, contains working samples, pattern/swatch selection, choice of price charts, order forms and initial supply of consumer literature for a number of product lines. Seven units, some 17½ in. wide, the other 27½ in. wide, can be installed in any combination desired by the retailer.

ADVERTISER: Hoyne
Steve Strasevicz, Director of Sales and Marketing
PRODUCER: Creative Displays Inc.

This wire stand shows off the product, making it easy for the customer to make a selection.

ADVERTISER: Mannington Mills
Robert Hennessey
PRODUCER: A.G. Industries Inc.
Vance Dimmick, Designer

This 30 ft. unit holds 272 floor covering samples, each 18 × 24 in., all visible in part at all times, but each can be easily removed for further examination. The computer unit, one of the first of its kind in the industry, helps the customer make a selection.

ADVERTISER: Flooring Distributors
Mike Hart
PRODUCER: Multiplex Display Fixture Co.
George J. Buzkij, Designer

Customers can easily go through the samples of actual ceramic tiles held in this rack. Overhead illumination adds to the attractiveness of the tile, and the impact of the header. Literature racks are on the ends of the unit.

ADVERTISER: Coronet Carpets Inc.
James Brady, Vice President
Clare Fisher, Operations Manager
PRODUCER: CDA Industries

To permit customers to touch and feel the product, a necessity for
many products, especially carpets, the company had three
permanent floor stand displays developed, a single unit, a double
unit, and a waterfall unit. Bronze OMA 1983.

ADVERTISER: Hoboken Wood Flooring Corp.
Richard Stennick, Sales Manager
PRODUCER: Melrose Displays Inc.
John Schlegel and Richard Stennick, Designers

Using only 9 sq. ft., this unit displays 30 samples of flooring, each
of which can be removed for examination, and replaced easily as
new patterns become available. Bronze OMA 1983.

ADVERTISER: Fiberglass Canada Inc.
PRODUCER: Gorrie Advertising Services

This kit, designed to support a contest, used a basic design on a wide variety of pieces, from small decals to large window posters. Local support was encouraged by including art for use in local advertising.

ADVERTISER: Formco Inc.
R. L. Koppana
PRODUCER: Multiplex Display Fixture Co.
George J. Buzkij, Designer

This floor-standing display allows the customer to examine 12 large product samples, while the descriptive panel holds full color photographs of room settings, product literature, and a list of benefits.

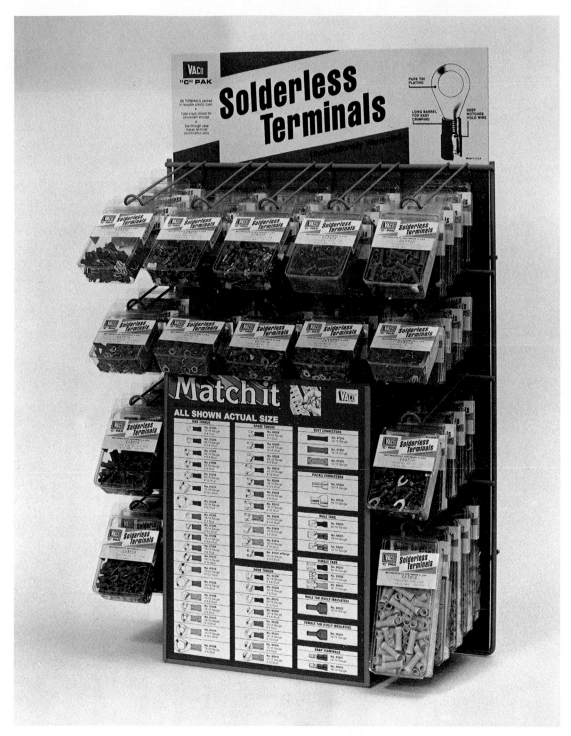

ADVERTISER: Vaco Products Co.
Craig Katz
PRODUCER: Wiremasters Inc.
J. M. Scriba Jr., Designer

An essentially unglamorous product is displayed attractively by this counter unit. The merchandise self-feeds; the central panel explains the uses and applications of the product; and the header sign calls attention to the product features.

ADVERTISER: Credo, Omark Industries
Bill Whitehead, Marketing Product Manager
PRODUCER: Wiremasters Inc.
J. M. Scriba Jr., Designer

In order to introduce an all-new, and expensive, product line, this sophisticated steel cabinet was developed. While it would usually be wall-mounted, it was stable enough to be placed on a sales counter. The clear acrylic door maintains high product visibility, but deters pilferage. First place winner, National Hardware Association show, 1982.

ADVERTISER: American Lock Co.
Al Vancura
PRODUCER: Wiremasters Inc.
J. M. Scriba Jr., Designer

This counter-top unit permits an actual test of a high security locking bolt, using a simulated wooden door section.

ADVERTISER: Silicone Products Division, General Electric Co.
Rich Vacarro, Manager, Consumer Marketing Programs
PRODUCER: A.G. Industries Inc.
John Vlah, Designer

To handle the demands of stores of all sizes, and yet offer a uniform appearance throughout, the designer developed several modules which could be assembled in a variety of configurations. The simplest has two shelves and a header, intended to be placed on a gondola shelf. A second module can be placed under the first, adding two shelves. For a free-standing unit, add an 8 in. base module. For increased capacity, the vertical module with a pegboard back can be added, with or without a base.

ADVERTISER: York, Borg-Warner Canada Ltd.
Martin Whelan, General Manager
Bill Bowen, Supervisor, Marketing Operations
PRODUCER: CDA Industries Inc.

Using a new company logo, this three-piece series gives dealers a simple way to identify themselves. All three items carry the five-color logo, and are illuminated. Bronze OMA 1983.

ADVERTISER: ExSil Spray & Lube, General Electric Co.
Rich Vacarro, Manager, Consumer Marketing Programs
Bill Driscoll, National Sales Manager
PRODUCER: AG Industries Inc.

This display, whose top mimics a can of lubricant, holds 144 cans of the product in only two square feet. Bronze OMA 1983.

ADVERTISER: 3M Co.
Duncan Russell, Marketing Supervisor
Adrian denTex, Package Design Coordinator
PRODUCER: Erickson Displays

This revolving floorstand has 30 sq. ft. of merchandising area in a floor space only 30 in. square. The headers help lead the customer to the right product line, while smaller decals guide him to the specific items he needs for the job in hand.

ADVERTISER: Easco/K-D Tools
Peter D. Scudner, Adv. & Sales Pro. Manager
DESIGNER: Herbst, Lazar, Rogers & Bell Inc.
Whitney Harkelroad, Designer
PRODUCER: Jovac Inc.

This merchandiser concentrates attention on the tools rather than
the display, believed to be an innovation in this industry.

This simple counter stand was used to introduce a brand new concept in lighting, by showing the bulb and permitting it to be turned on as a demonstration. Copy on the top explained its special features, while a map spelled out actual savings in key cities. The foil lining of the recess adds additional impact. Bronze OMA 1983.

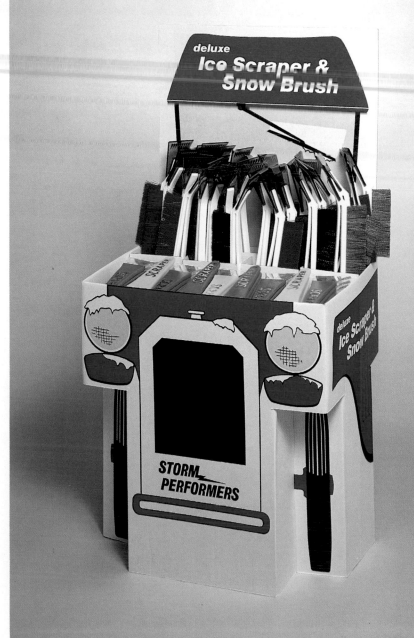

Suggesting its use by its design, this corrugated floor stand makes the product easy to buy on impulse.

POPPOPPOPPOP
POPPOPPOPPOPPOP
POPPOPPOPPOPPOP
POPPOPPOPPOPPOPPOP
POPPOPPOPPOPPOP
POPPOPPOPPOPPOPP
POPPOPPOPPOPPO
POPPOPPOPPOPP
POPPOPPOPPO

5

Farm, Agricultural and Garden Supplies

This is probably the smallest section in this book, and the reason is simple. It is undoubtedly the least active, in a promotional sense, of the categories into which American industry has been divided by the Point-of-Purchase Advertising Institute.

It is hard to know why this category of products should be so different from others we have covered. It really includes two distinct markets. The first is the market of the full-time farmer, the agricultural producer, the professional. These consumers are very similar in their thought processes to industrial consumers, and in general, this is an area that does not utilize point-of-purchase to move the market closer to the buying decision. The professional farmer uses other sources of information to help him make up his mind. He reads his professional journals; he confers with his county agent; he talks to his friends and neighbors. He is not likely to have his mind changed by a display which greets him when he arrives at his dealer's.

On the other hand, the amateur farmer, the suburban gardener, the flower-growing housewife, are quite different. These people do not have the time, nor the need, to weigh their decisions as carefully as the professional. The economics of their purchase is not as essential to their livelihood as with the full-time farmer. They can afford to try, and they enjoy trying, new chemicals, new tools, new techniques. They are obviously more easily moved by p.o.p. advertising.

Yet all the challenges that face p.o.p. in other areas occur in this one, too. The designer must meet the needs of the outlets in which his units are to be placed; he must attract the attention of the shopper and get his message across; he must stay within his budget, and since total volume is usually less than with more widely distributed categories, he may find this a more difficult task.

POPPOPPOPPOPPOPPOP
POPPOPPOPPOPPOP
POPPOPPOPPOPPOP
POPPOPPOPPOP
POPPOPPOPPOPPOP
POPPOPPOPPOP
POPPOPPOPPOPPOP
POPPOPPOPPOP
POPPOPPOPPOP
POPPOPPOPPOP
POPPOPPOPPOP

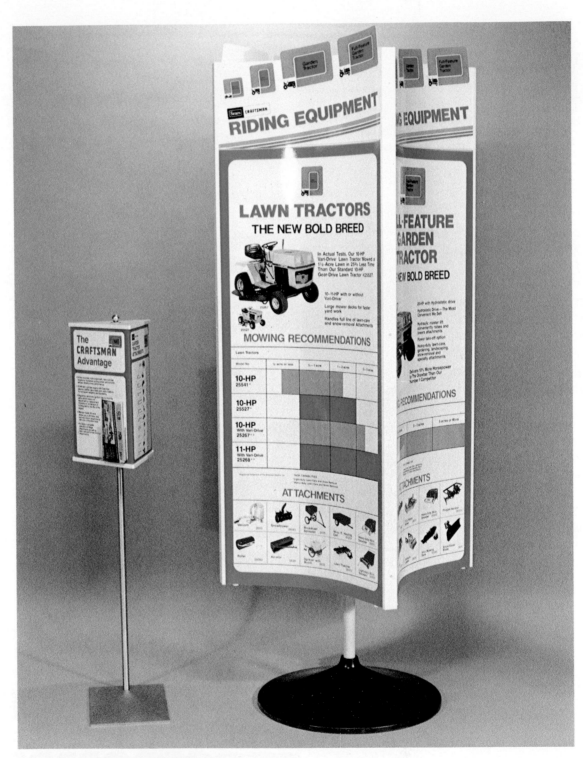

ADVERTISER: Sears, Roebuck and Company
Lee Schwartz, National Display Manager
PRODUCER: Frank Mayer and Associates Inc.

This free-standing piece is often the focal point of the lawn and gardening department, since it furnishes an excellent starting point for a prospect considering the purchase of one of these expensive items. Its detailed listing of product features helps to differentiate to various price levels and make them meaningful. Bronze OMA 1983.

ADVERTISER: General Electric Co.
Joe Sbrocco, Specialist, Sales Merchandising
PRODUCER: Creative Displays Inc.

This lamp center for indoor gardens uses a rustic wood finish to suggest living plants, and the bright yellow has a suggestion of the sunlight.

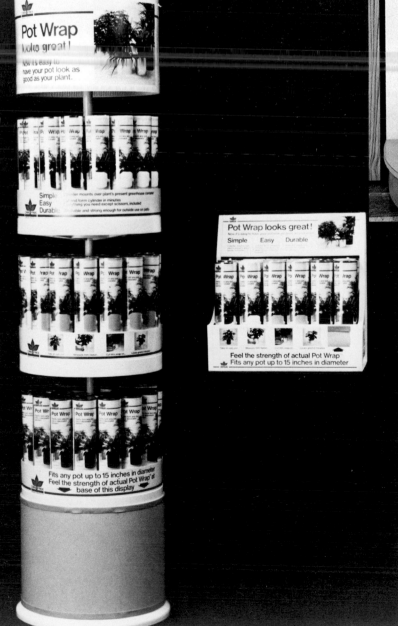

ADVERTISER: JPA Company
Joel Farrell, President
Edward Swallow, Marketing Manager
PRODUCER: Burke Communication Industries

The floor display holds six dozen product packages, and itself reminds the viewer of a package. Through graphics and copy, the unit shows how easy the item is to use and how attractive it makes the pot. The related counter unit, for smaller outlets, holds two dozen packages. Bronze OMA 1983.

ADVERTISER: Greenview, division of Lebanon Chemical
Gene Wright
PRODUCER: Display Technologies
Dick Osgood Designer

Because of its size, this display commands an end aisle position. To accommodate the weight of the product, two wooden slats are used to support each shelf.

ADVERTISER: Morton-Thiokol Co.
Bruce Barfield, VP, Sales
Jack Thomas, Brand Manager
PRODUCER: Design Promotions

Molded in black styrene, this unit has clear legs supporting the upper three shelves, and black legs supporting the base. It moves this product out of the usual, dull wire rack, and organizes it in an aesthetically pleasing merchandiser. Bronze OMA 1983.

ADVERTISER: Velsicol Chemical Corp.
Vincent Mazza, Director of Advertising
PRODUCER: Visual Marketing Inc.
Phillip L. Marco, Designer

This promotional program included a quartz battery clock, a multi-image window card, measuring rule, and imprinted ball-point pens.
Bronze OMA 1982

ADVERTISER: Hudson
PRODUCER: Creative Displays Inc.

This self-standing floor unit organizes bulky equipment into a department of its own. The three-dimensional awning suggests immediately yard and garden use.

ADVERTISER: O.M. Scott & Sons
PRODUCER: Anglo Affiliated Co.

This inflatable unit drew attention in a most graphic way to the undesirable presence of dandelions, and suggested the Scott product as a remedy.

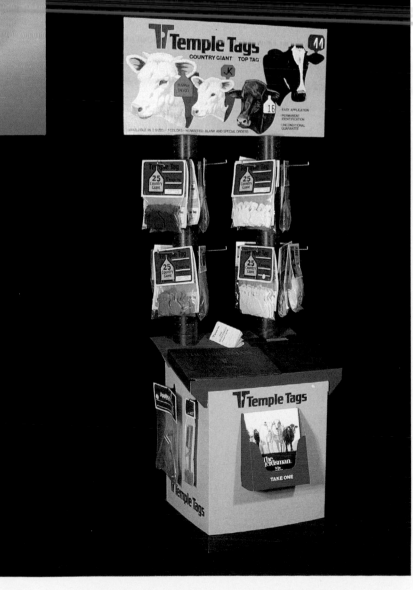

ADVERTISER: Temple Tags, Zoecon Industries
Jayne Kysar, Packaging Supervisor
PRODUCER: E. and E. Specialties
Nelson Orwig, Designer

This semi-permanent display stores and shows an entire line of cattle identification products, taking up the minimum floor space. Bronze OMA 1979.

6

Transportation

When we move into this category after spending some time in the environment of the supermarket, we seem to enter an entirely different world. Not that selling automobiles or gasoline is any less competitive. Certainly the battle of the brands is as intense in the world of the automobile as in the world of processed food. And when you consider the marketing of petroleum products, you begin to realize that here is a product that the consumer never sees, has no recognizable physical characteristics, where one brand is indistinguishable from another, and where the consumer decision must be based on image. The creation of image is almost entirely the function of advertising, including point-of-purchase.

In the new-car showroom, p.o.p. advertising plays a different role. While image is a key factor, the surrounding circumstances are different. The prospective buyer, with a substantial investment in mind, enters the showroom with an interest in a particular brand. His brand preference has been created by his own experience, by the experience of others (obtained either by reading or by talking to other car owners) and by national advertising. Now he comes to see for himself, to find out his specific options, and to compare what he would like against what is available, and if satisfied, to make his final decisions.

In the new-car industry, point-of-purchase falls into three broad categories. The first is the more or less permanent signing that identifies the dealership. This is simply to identify the dealer as one of the family of dealerships that handles a specific brand. The second, also designed to be seen from the outside, is temporary. It highlights a specific promotion, hoping to entice the prospect into the showroom, giving him a good reason to pay an immediate visit. It may, perhaps, pick up on a theme from the manufacturer's national promotion. Finally, there are displays that are designed to bring information to the prospect, with or without the assistance of a salesperson. These may consist of explanations of special mechanical features, or they may make it easier to select from optional color and fabric schemes and thus take some of the confusion out of the myriad of options.

This interior point-of-purchase display material offers ample opportunity to the designer. They are generally long lasting, designed to be used throughout a model year. For this reason, they must be made of more rugged materials, and the advertiser can afford to spend a little more to achieve this longevity. These displays must also project the air of luxury and solidity that the manufacturer and dealer wish to apply to the car itself. Finally, the lack of competitive brand displays permits the designer a degree of subtlety and perhaps of understatement that is difficult

to resort to in more competitive situations. In general, the group of interior display units intended to be used in showrooms of new automobiles can reach a high level of both engineering technology and design.

Like new-car dealers, the service station is tied almost exclusively to a brand whose presence dominates the location. The consumer builds up a sort of loyalty to a brand, and wants to know where he can get his favorite gas. Since he is usually traveling down the highway when he enters a buying situation, he must be able to recognize a supplier at a distance. Point-of-purchase displays offer this kind of identification at a distance, and the whole location carries out this identification theme. Temporary p.o.p. is used to help the dealer increase his volume, to encourage the sale of other items besides gasoline. Manufacturers of tires, batteries, and accessories also design displays that work toward the same objective, and those selling displays are often the reason why dealers select one brand over another.

The designer of displays for the travel industry faces a split objective. His work will be seen in controlled situations, as in downtown airline ticket offices, and in

uncontrolled ones, as in travel agency offices. In the former, the display units are often the only items that catch the eye. They will be seen because they are there. There will be no material from competitive carriers to distract the eye or give a competing message.

When the designer moves into the office of a travel agency, he faces an entirely different situation. An agency represents many suppliers, and every airline, every cruise line, almost every destination wishes to call attention to itself; many travel agencies will accept whatever is offered, as long as it has some appeal to its patrons, and will put it somewhere. The net result is a frightful competition for attention, and often there is no winner.

ADVERTISER: Cadillac Motor Car Division, General Motors Corp.
Frank Cadicamo, Asst. Dir. of Merchandising
Constance Carruthers, Sales Promotion Manager
PRODUCER: DCI Marketing

This self-standing unit is designed to stand near a display car. To operate the unit, the prospect presses an identified button to illuminate the appropriate picture and copy. Interior and exterior color selections are also included.

ADVERTISER: Cadillac Motor Car Division, General Motors Corp.
Frank Cadicamo, Asst. Dir. of Merchandising
Constance Carruthers, Sales Promotion Manager
PRODUCER: DCI Marketing

Promoting the youthful sports car image of the Cimarron, the showroom display, package included front end protector, sheepskin seat covers, luggage rack and cargo box. A direct mailing to all owners offered 20 items for purchase. Bronze OMA 1983.

ADVERTISER: G.M. Photographic, General Motors Corp.
Jim Oehlberg, Marketing Planner
Jim McDonald, Administrator, Creative Art
PRODUCER: Frank Mayer & Associates Inc.

This unusual literature holder is a colorful replica of the Chevy Blazer, which can sit right on top of the vehicle being sold. Bronze OMA 1983.

ADVERTISER: BMW of North America Inc.
Peter Mantia, Carol Brust
PRODUCER: Einson Freeman Inc.
Designer: Gary Bobcik

These elegant floor stands, with their simple yet luxurious design, places the BMW above all competitive imported luxury sports cars. Blow-ups of current advertising can be used, along with a selection of brochures. Ninety-five percent of all target dealers have purchased the program. Bronze OMA 1983.

ADVERTISER: BMW of North America Inc.
Peter Mantia, Natl. Purchasing Agent
Robert D. Mitchell, Advertising & Promotion Manager/Motorcycles

PRODUCER: Display Systems Inc.

The two-sided display is designed to help establish a BMW department in the dealer's showroom, which may carry several brands, often out-numbering the BMW models on the floor. One side holds literature, the other a changeable poster. If desired, the two pieces can be removed from the pole and mounted on the wall.

ADVERTISER: Mazda Motors of America
Howard D. Caudle, Sales Promotion Manager
PRODUCER: DCI Marketing

This cylindrical unit attracts attention with its colorful graphics, while information booklets are easily available in the racks. The carpeted base serves as a storage cabinet for additional booklets. Bronze OMA 1983.

ADVERTISER: Puch Bicycles
PRODUCER: Ridan Displays
John Gross, Designer

This wall-mounted display can be supplied in either 26 or 38 inch sizes, with or without a clock. Bronze OMA 1982.

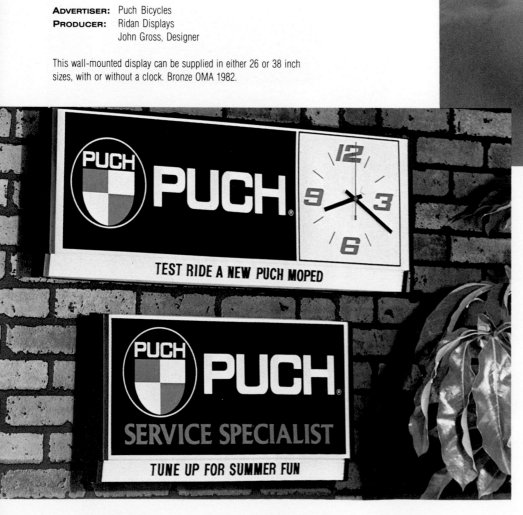

ADVERTISER: Suzuki Canada Ltd.
Rick Suzuki, President
PRODUCER: CDA Industries Inc.

Provides a complete program for dealers to introduce a new four-wheel drive car, tying in with the total national advertising program. Inserts can be changed to up-date or to meet local concerns.

ADVERTISER: American Honda Motor Car Inc.
Eric Kahn, Director of Advertising
PRODUCER: Continental Graphics
Colin Bedding, Design Director

This pleasing stand is compact, and makes it easy for the customer to find all the information he needs in one spot. The slanted surface holds photos and text about each model, while descriptive literature is in a near-by pocket. A color book is in its own compartment, and the technical data book, which also held comparative data on other makes, is on the slanted top. The unit rotates for easy use.

ADVERTISER: Nissan Automobile Co. (Canada) Ltd.
Robert Thurston, Merchandising Supervisor
PRODUCER: CDA Industries Inc.

This floor stand helps the customer choose the interior and exterior colors available for each model. New kits can be used to replace old ones to keep up with annual model changes.

ADVERTISER: Cadillac Motor Car Division, General Motors Corp.
Frank Cadicamo, Asst. Dir. of Merchandising
Constance Carruthers, Sales Promotion Manager
PRODUCER: DCI Marketing

This pedestal presents a computerized message with entertaining graphics that lets copy explode, flash, reverse, or fade on or off. A hand-held programmer permits the dealer to add his own message and to customize the graphics. Bronze OMA 1983.

ADVERTISER: Cadillac Motor Car Division, General Motors Corp.
Frank Cadicamo, Asst. Dir. of Merchandising
Constance Carruthers, Sales Promotion Manager
PRODUCER: DCI Marketing

This single book, combining exterior color and interior upholstery selections, replaced two separate books used in prior years, cutting cost by 30% and simplifying the sales force learning process. Silver OMA 1983.

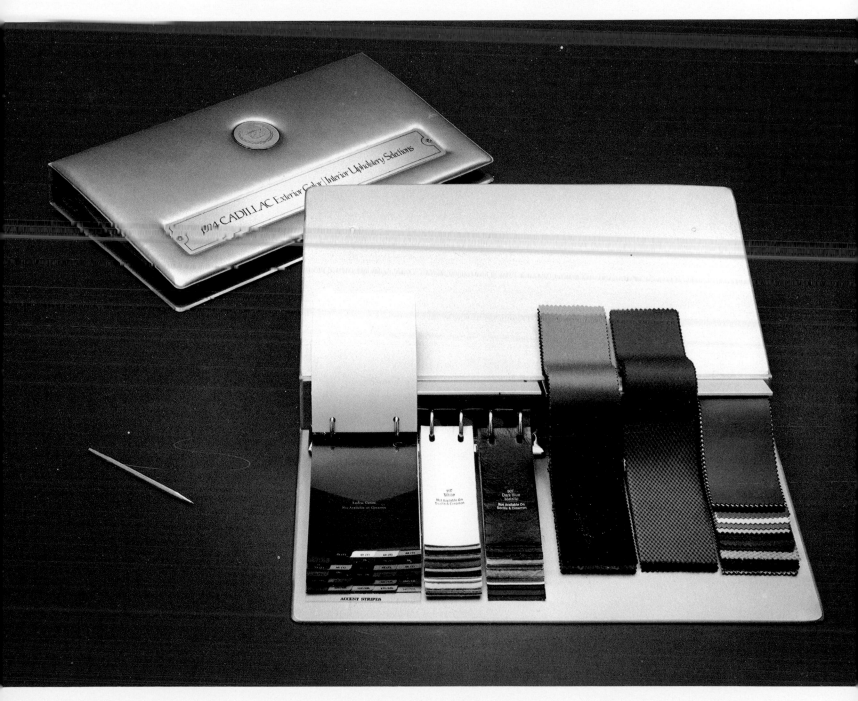

ADVERTISER: Champion Spark Plug Co.
Larry Wilson, Administrator, Special Account Merchandising
Tony Thiros, Production Manager
PRODUCER: The Hennegan Co.

This shelf-talker, printed on clear acetate and folded to bring a product replica perpendicular to the shelf, reminds the customer at the moment of purchase that Champion is a leader. Bronze OMA 1983.

ADVERTISER: Generic
PRODUCER: Benchmarc Display Inc.

This unit, of high-impact plastic, is designed to display any automobile tire, regardless of width or size. It is made of two identical injection-molded parts.

ADVERTISER: Kelsey Products Div. Kelsey-Hayes Co.
M. McGrath, Sales Manager
B. McNutt, Manager Marketing Services
PRODUCER: Benchmarc Display Inc.

A new feature in this industry permitted the wheels to be easily removed for close inspection. The display holds more than 75% of the available styles. Bronze OMA 1983

ADVERTISER: Walker Mufflers, Tenneco Automotive
Mike Sucharda, Director of Marketing
Harvey Diedrich, Sales Promotion Manager
PRODUCER: DCI Marketing

This display was used primarily to get P.O.P. in the highly competitive display areas of auto parts stores. If the dealer bought a permanent display piece, he would get his own personalized chair, along with a customer offer. If the dealer also sent in a photo of the display in use, he would get one free muffler, whose sale would liquidate the cost of the original display. Bronze OMA 1983.

ADVERTISER: Hella lamps, Bosal Canada Ltd.
Colin Payne, Managing Director
PRODUCER: CDA Industries Inc.

This compact unit enables the customer to compare the lights, since each may be turned on and off for an actual demonstration.

ADVERTISER: Walker Exhaust
Hugh McKeown
PRODUCER: Gorrie Advertising Services

Posters and entry blanks were used to promote this prize offer, but most unusual was the entry deposit box, which used the bicycle to be awarded as the floor stand.

ADVERTISER: Ford of Canada
Ron Elliott, Marketing Plans Manager
PRODUCER: CDA Industries Inc.

In limited space, this unit calls attention to a hidden feature, encouraging customers to take a test drive. Omission of date permitted the display to be used for two model years.

ADVERTISER: Monroe Shocks, Tenneco Automotive
Harvey P. Diedrich, Sales Promotion Manager
PRODUCER: Benchmarc Display Inc.

The central post of this floor display is a replica of the product, for instant product recognition.

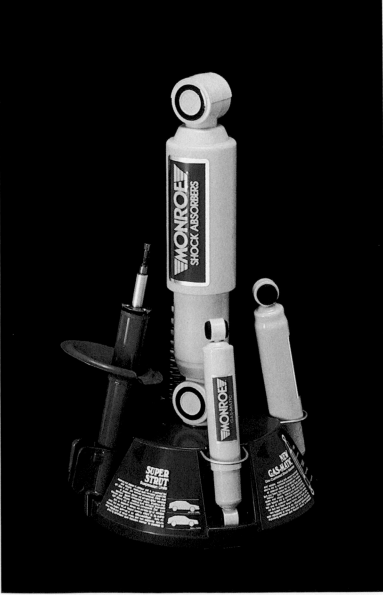

ADVERTISER: Monroe Shocks, Tenneco Automotive
James Lietaert
PRODUCER: Benchmarc Display Inc.

A replica of the product serves as the center post of this counter stool, which was compatible with the service desk.

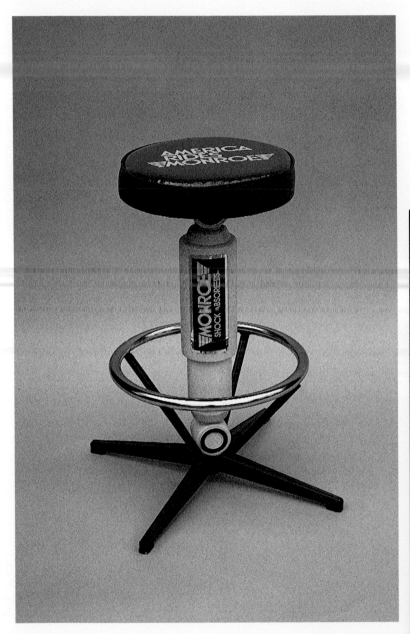

ADVERTISER: Monroe Shocks, Tenneco Automotive
Harvey P. Diedrich, Sales Promotion Manager
PRODUCER: Benchmarc Display Inc.

The two-tiered revolving shelf permits the maximum amount of product in the minimum space.

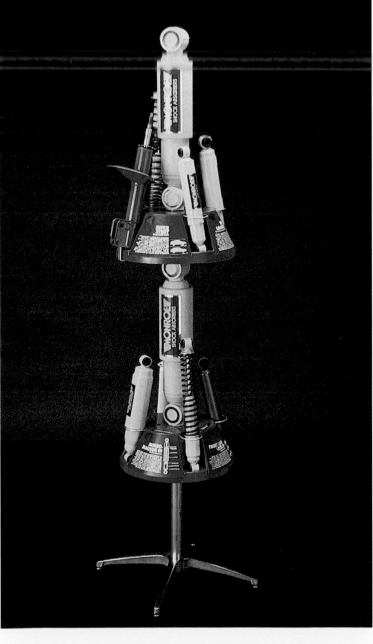

ADVERTISER: Eastern Auto Sound
George Waffer
PRODUCER: Miller Manufacturing Inc.

Impressions ABA
Industries Inc., Designer

This free-standing display tower serves as a demonstrator for three
car radio models. Gold OMA 1982.

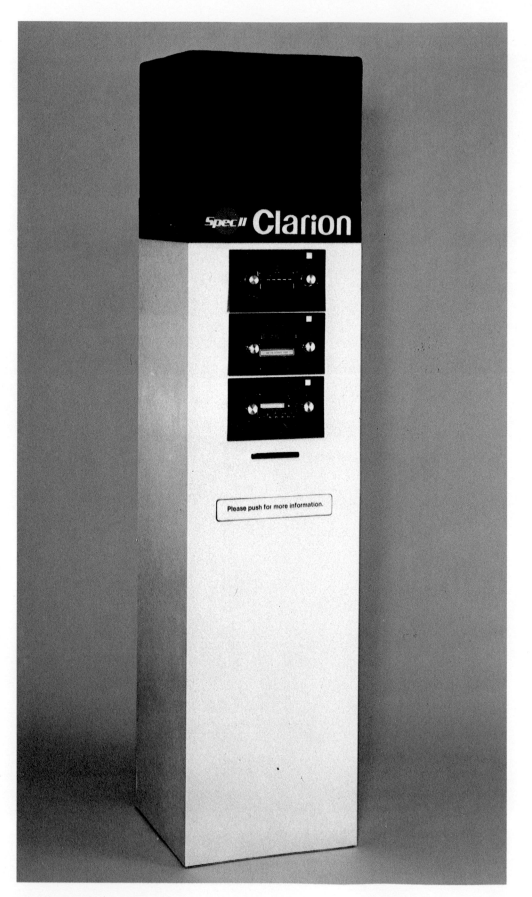

ADVERTISER: Delco Electronic, General Motors Corp.
John Reeder
PRODUCER: DCI Marketing

This free-standing unit permits prospects to compare sound and handling of automobile sound systems. Colorful back panels assist sales personnel in merchandising the units.

ADVERTISER: Car Stereo Subsidiary, Sony Corp of America
Jim Geitz, Advertising Manager
Andy Swensen, Technical Services Manager
PRODUCER: MKB Group Inc.

Designed to introduce a new concept, the unit uses bold graphics and sequential flashing lights to call attention to itself. Once attracted, the prospect is told how the unit works in and out of the car, and can give himself a demonstration. Special care was given to the location, angle, and acoustical baffling of the four operational speakers. All components are mounted to prevent theft, but not hamper the unit at work. Bronze OMA 1983.

ADVERTISER: Exxon Co. USA, Exxon Corp.
James Stanislaus, Advertising Manager
Peter Mantell, Marketing Specialist

PRODUCER: DINACO Inc.

This is a total program that includes window posters, streamers, standing posters, and pump toppers. Standard items are supplemented by seasonal ones, and individual packages built around a single product category, and tied in with advertising specialties and national television. Gold OMA 1983.

ADVERTISER: Valvoline
John K. Voight, Senior Artist
Dennis Steinhofer, Manager, Advertising Services
PRODUCER: The Dyment Co.
Gary Wilkins , Designer

The enlarged replica of the product is powered by a solar motor. The rotation of the can and the dangling of the copy card catch the eye. Bronze OMA 1983.

ADVERTISER: Gulf Canada
PRODUCER: Gorrie Advertising Services
Paul Whittington, Designer

This molded polyethylene carrier, unlike metal, will not dent, rust or chip. The back panel can be used to mount an advertising message. With a color change, it was sold to many Canadian oil companies.

ADVERTISER: U-Haul International Inc.
Jim Shaw, Marketing Director
AGENCY: A. & M. Associates
Gary Robertson
PRODUCER: International Patterns Inc.

U-Haul wanted to convey more information to a client as he waited to order his equipment, to save the time of the salesperson. These grooved boards were developed to hold both panels and letters, which fit into the grooves. The panels, of varying widths, could be silk screened.

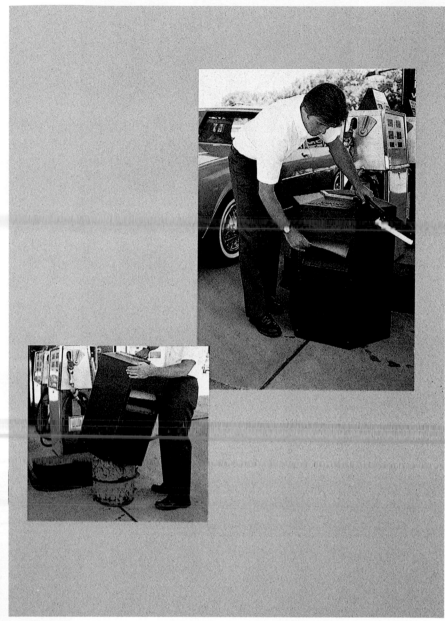

ADVERTISER: Amoco, Standard Oil of Indiana
Jim Stowasser, Staff Buyer
PRODUCER: DCI Marketing

To help reduce the clutter on gas station islands, this attractive unit was offered to retailers. Bronze OMA 1983.

ADVERTISER: Mr. Goodwrench, General Motors Corp.
PRODUCER: Stout Industries Inc.

This life-size figure, made of aluminum for durability, can be attached to a wall or, as shown here, mounted on a wheeled floor stand. Special signs can be placed in position, each with pockets for price changes. Bronze OMA.

ADVERTISER: Kellogg Company
Ken Kropen, Manager of Promotion Services

PRODUCER: Johnstons and Associates
Beth Schroeder, Designer

A hanging store display features a die-cut United Airlines 747 under a rainbow, plus replicas of the four participating products. Supporting materials used the same design elements, and the promotion was featured in airline ticket offices and travel agencies, as well as in supermarkets.

ADVERTISER: United Airlines
John Wyer, Visual Merchandising Manager
PRODUCER: Burke Communication Industries

This colorful unit takes up little space and attracts attention with the up-and-down motion of the arm, and the side-to-side motion of the head. Bronze OMA, 1983.

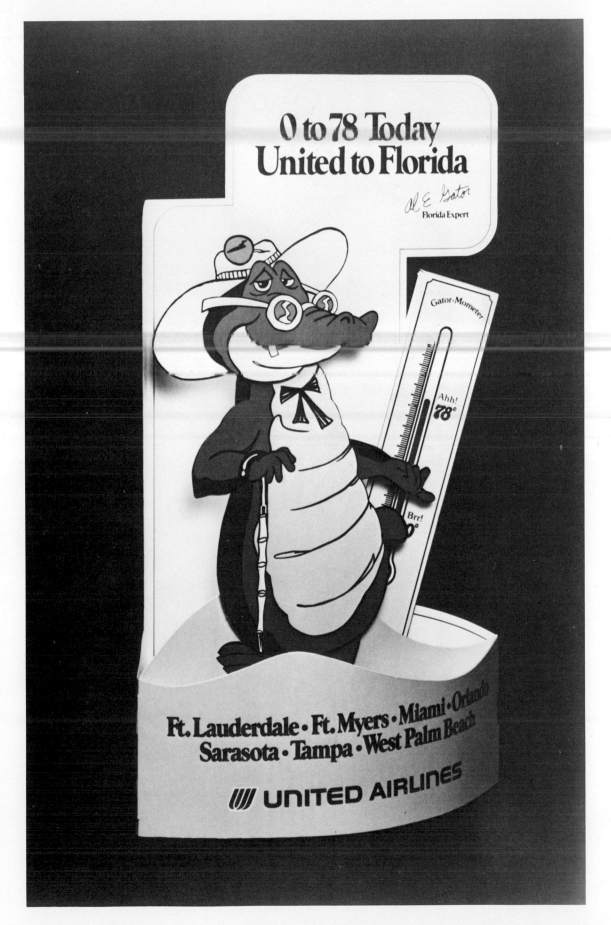

ADVERTISER: American Airlines
PRODUCER: Great Northern Corporation

An extremely versatile display, the hexagonal units can be put together in many configurations.

ADVERTISER: Air Canada
PRODUCER: Gorrie Advertising Services

These decorative posters were mounted back to back, with a spacer to hold them in a gentle curve, making them self-standing. Their low cost made it possible to distribute freely. They shipped flat for savings, but were easily turned into their three-dimensional aspect.

ADVERTISER: USAir Inc.
Suzanne Cochran, Sales Promotion Manager
PRODUCER: IDL Inc.

Designed for city ticket offices, this modular unit makes it simple to change price and destination panels.

POPPOPPOPPOP
POPPOPPOPPOPPOP
POPPOPPOPPOPPOP
POPPOPPOPPOPPOPPOP
POPPOPPOPPOPPOP
POPPOPPOPPOPF
POPPOPPOPPOPPO
POPPOPPOPPOPP
POPPOPPOPPO

7
Beverages

Of all the industries included in this book, perhaps none presents a greater challenge to the point-of-purchase designer than beverages. There are several reasons for this, and not all of them are apparent to those who are not involved in its problems.

There are two distinct divisions within this category, since it includes non-alcoholic soft drinks on the one hand, and alcoholic beverages, including beer, wine, and hard spirits, on the other. The non-alcoholic segment includes, although it may often be overlooked, simple water. In point of fact, more water, both tap and bottled, is consumed than any other type of beverage. And in recent years, bottled water has been increasing its share of market, largely due to promotion. While different, all kinds of beverages must be considered together, since they all share the quality of satisfying thirst. However, their distribution channels are so varied that they can hardly be discussed in the same terms.

Soft drinks are products that probably have the widest variety of distribution of all. They are sold in supermarkets, in convenience stores; they are sold at room temperature and refrigerated; they come with and without sugar; in bottles and cans; in various sizes. They are even sold in vending machines which can be in motels, service stations, office buildings, and anywhere else where there is traffic.

Soft drinks are heavily advertised through radio, television, magazines. They utilize couponing, premiums, rebates, contests, sweepstakes, in a bewildering series of promotions that follow one after the other. Point-of-purchase advertising plays a big role in soft-drink promotion. The volume is so great that the bottlers fight for even a small increase in market penetration, and the soft-drink companies find that point-of-purchase can make the difference. Symbolizing this impact, perhaps, is the display for Pepsi-Cola, winner of a gold OMA, in which a six-pack of the product seems to tip off the shelf by itself. The natural impulse of anybody within reach of the tipping package is to reach out and grab.

The fact that the product category has achieved such wide distribution means that the average production of a p.o.p unit is comparatively large. This in turn leads to a lower cost per unit and permits the designer to use materials and techniques that might be out of reach in shorter runs.

When we move from soft drinks to beer, wine, and liquor, we move into a totally different and often bewildering world. There is certainly competition in these products, and it is often intense competition. While every bottler tries to build brand loyalty, this is difficult to achieve and maintain. The competition among products is mirrored by the competition among bottlers, competition for attention and display space. That is why so many display units in this field are built around some function that is considered desirable by the store

proprietor, or that tries to find a space that is not preempted. Examples of this are menu or price boards for retailers or taverns, clocks, and so on.

But the major factor that is so bewildering to one who has not been active in this category is the multiplicity of state and local restrictions on promotional activity. Some states, known as control states, permit no privately owned liquor stores, but sell only through state-owned and -operated outlets; in other states, known as license states, these stores are privately owned. In some jurisdictions, wine and beer can be sold in supermarkets; in others it is limited to specialized outlets only.

In addition, there is a long list of restrictions on what can be done in the way of promotion, and it may vary from one community to its neighbor—although it is true that most requirements are statewide. Some of these restrictions are very detailed. For example, a state may specify the maximum number of square inches that may be used in a display unit. An apocryphal story goes that during the discussion of this limitation by one state's liquor commission, one member insisted that no product needed more than a page of the New York *Times* to tell its story. So a page of the newspaper was measured, and that number of square inches was written into state regulations as the maximum size for a liquor store display. No consideration was given to the economics of production, the space

needed for efficient functioning, or the effects of size on store management. A neighboring state, using another decision factor, may have settled on a limitation of six square inches more, or six square inches less. Some states restrict the use of light, or of motion, while one or both may be permitted in other locations. Some states place a limit on the value of a promotion piece, or prohibit the inclusion of a useful accessory.

There is no question that this multiplicity of regulations is a burden on the industry as a whole, and on the point-of-purchase designer and producer. Nothing can be manufactured and distributed without taking into account the current local regulations. The market area for a specific brand must be defined; the regulations which pertain must be studied; the proposed display weighed against the pertinent rules.

With all these restrictions, the output is remarkably high in quality. Displays are attractive and ingenious, and the ideas they include are often picked up and transferred to other fields.

ADVERTISER: Miller Brewing Co.
Don Frank, Art Director
Doug Rogers, Brand Manager
PRODUCER: Everbrite Electric Signs Inc.

Not only is this piece handsome, but it has been designed for simple installation, which adds to its attractiveness for the distributor and retailer. It is also simple to change the brand identification and slogan. Gold OMA 1983.

ADVERTISER: Molson, Martlet Importing Co. Inc.
Robert C. Ringer, Merchandising Manager
PRODUCER: Bob Robinson Marketing Inc.

Fine art work makes this unit a dramatic eye-catcher. Produced at low cost without sacrificing quality, the torso is made of dyed paper cell material, light enough to pick up transient air currents. The wings are four-color printing on tag stock. Silver OMA 1983.

ADVERTISER: Molson, Martlet Importing Co. Inc.
Robert C. Ringer, Merchandising Manager
PRODUCER: Bob Robinson Marketing Inc.

A 5 ft. tall plastic replica of a bottle of Molson's is used as the backdrop for the product. The bottle half can also be mounted on the wall, or placed back-to-back for a full-round display. Bronze OMA 1982.

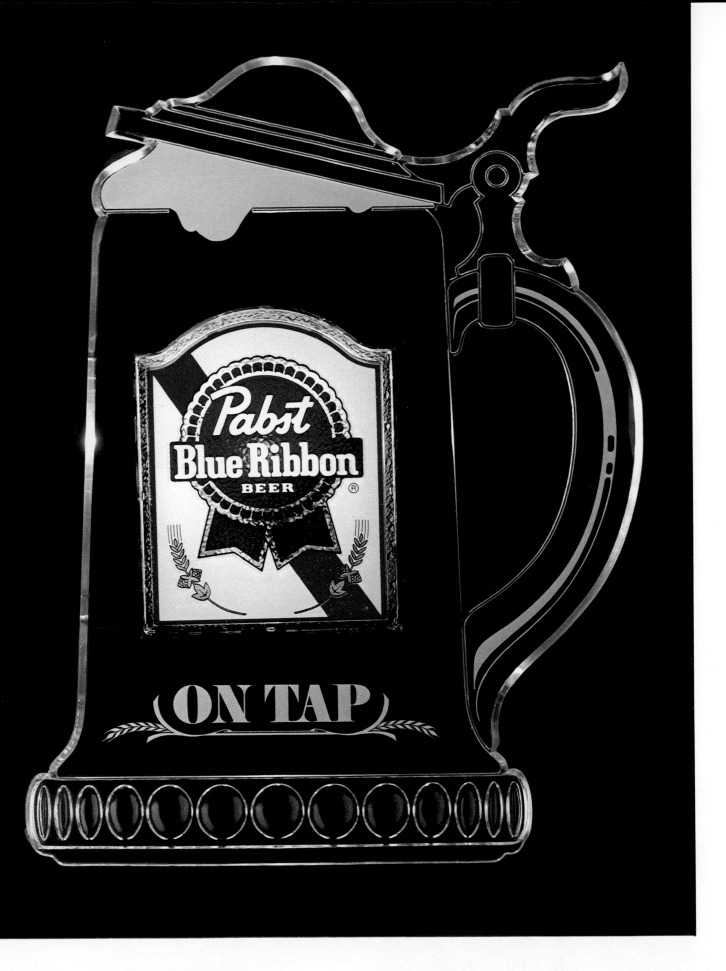

ADVERTISER: Pabst Brewery
Lou Saksefski, Manager, Creative Services
Stanley K. Kovach, Director of Marketing Services
PRODUCER: KCS Industries Inc.

In a cluttered bar environment, this sign's simple lines and avoidance of busy colors makes it a standout. The subtle illumination is achieved with a small incandescent bulb. Bronze OMA 1983.

ADVERTISER: Pabst Brewery
Lou Saksefski, Manager, Creative Services
Stanley K. Kovach, Director of Marketing Services
PRODUCER: KCS Industries Inc.

The elegance of this classical piece, which looked like stained glass, brought it a greater than expected level of market acceptance.

ADVERTISER: Pabst Brewery
Lou Saksefski, Manager, Creative Services
Stanley K. Kovach, Director of Marketing Services
PRODUCER: Thomas A. Schutz Co.

The unique pricing panel of this display resembles electronic digits, but without the expense. The numbering is indexed to make it easy to change prices, with no pieces to loosen or fall off, and no storage of numbers. Bronze OMA 1983.

ADVERTISER: Adolph Coors Co.
Robert Hobbs, Group Manager,
Merchandising Promotions Licensing
Marc Barrios, Group Manager, Credit Services
PRODUCER: KCS Industries Inc.

Coors set out to develop a refrigerator sign series to provide full line support. Modular units make the display flexible. The large panels can use supportive graphics or a pricing panel with digital figures. Other units can have digital clocks, or programmable messages. Bronze OMA 1983.

ADVERTISER: Adolph Coors Brewing Co.
PRODUCER: Stout Industries Inc.

Standing 7 ft. high and 3 ft. across, this replica has plastic caps and can be bolted to a wall.

ADVERTISER: Olympia Brewing Co.
G. John Heelan, Point of Sale Manager
PRODUCER: Visual Marketing Inc.
Donald F. Buck, Designer

Made of injection molded plastic, with fluorescent illumination, this wall-mounted piece attracted attention with the lenticular animation of the waterfall. Bronze OMA 1982.

ADVERTISER: Budweiser, Anheuser Busch Inc.
Tom Thomas, Assoc. Sales Promotion Manager
PRODUCER: Visual Marketing Inc.
Dennis A. Nielson

Made of tag stock construction, this unit attracted attention with its changeable messages. Collateral material also broadened its impact. Bronze OMA 1982.

ADVERTISER: Bud Light, Anheuser-Busch Inc.
Zanvel Zack, Director, Creative Services
PRODUCER: Everbrite Electric Signs Inc.

Designed for back bar use, this unit uses a 6-watt fluorescent lamp in the base. Distinctive and elegant, it has received widespread acceptance. Bronze OMA 1983.

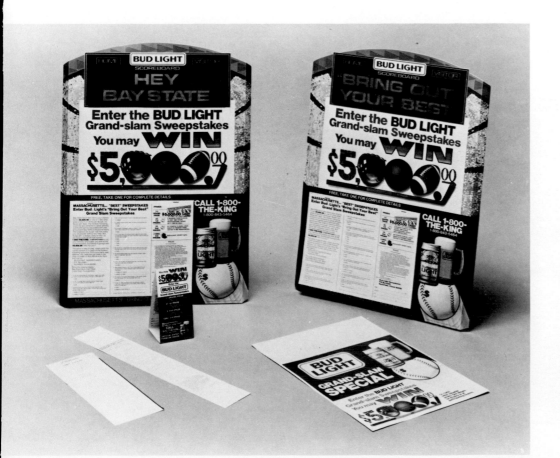

ADVERTISER: Bud Light, Anheuser-Busch Inc.
Tom Thomas, Associate Sales Promotion Manager
PRODUCER: Visual Marketing Inc.

A promotion limited to a single state used a plastic optigraphic panel to present a changing message. Entry blanks were on pads attached to the displays as well as on table tents. The correct answers could be obtained by calling a toll-free number, which gave not only the answers, but also an advertising message. Bronze OMA 1983.

ADVERTISER: Kirin Brewery, The Cherry Co.
PRODUCER: Thomson-Leeds Co. Inc.

In an effort to move from Japanese and Chinese restaurants into American ones, the advertiser wanted a promotional piece versatile enough to reflect its Japanese image, yet suitable for broader use. The solution was this back bar piece featuring the Kirin itself, a half-dragon, half-horse creature which, according to Chinese mythology, spawned the prophet Confucius. A light is incorporated in the base.

ADVERTISER: Michelob Light, Anheuser-Busch Inc.
Michael V. Roarty, VP, Marketing
Jack McDonough, VP, Brand Management
PRODUCER: John Stark Printing Co. Inc.

This pole stand attracts attention to a stack of product. Four changeable beer pictures permit the retailer to match the display to the variety he wishes to promote. The die-cut handle on the mug reaches out to the customer. Bronze OMA 1983.

ADVERTISER: Michelob Light, Anheuser-Busch Inc.
Michael V. Roarty, VP, Marketing
Jack McDonough, VP, Brand Management
PRODUCER: John Stark Printing Co. Inc.

Up to 8 cases of 12-ounce bottles can be stacked in the display, which is best used in areas of heavy traffic. The corrugated display picks up the colors and design of the six-pack, while the header has room for a local message. Bronze OMA 1983.

ADVERTISER: Löwenbräu, Miller Brewing Co.
David Hairopoulos, Administrator, Point-of-Sale
Lester Sentz, Senior Buyer
PRODUCER: DCI Marketing

The sign is available in an illuminated or unlit model. While generally engraved on clear plastic, a blue panel is supplied where the wall might be incompatible with the crystal clear sign. Bronze OMA 1983.

ADVERTISER: The Stroh's Brewery Co.
Thomas H. Sculthorpe, Merchandising Manager
PRODUCER: Visual Marketing Inc.
John F. Deffner, Designer

Alternating between red and green as it slowly revolved, this plastic lantern looks like expensive brass, and was welcomed as decoration in many taverns and lounges. Bronze OMA 1980.

ADVERTISER: St. Pauli Girl Beer, Carlton Brewing Co.
Robert Warrington, VP, Marketing
John Gregory
PRODUCER: Advertising Display Co.

To introduce a new brand, the company offered, without charge, a free poster. The floorstand contains 100 posters pre-packed into an easily set up display. Gold OMA 1983.

ADVERTISER: Ernest & Julio Gallo
Allen Berger, Marketing Manager
PRODUCER: Creative Displays Inc.

The warmth of wood, the colors of Fall, and a sunset photograph create a mood which encourages the purchase of wine. This display will handle a large amount of the product.

ADVERTISER: Ernest & Julio Gallo Winery
William DeGraw, Creative Director
PRODUCER: Container Corporation of America

The three-dimensional barrel frames a full-color photograph, and adds to the romance of the wine. Cut cases of wines selected by the retailer make it easy to make a purchase. Bronze OMA 1983.

ADVERTISER: Beringer Wines, Wine World Inc.
Jim Toujum, Director of Sales Promotion
PRODUCER: Great Northern Corporation Display Division

Two-tiered butcher block floor base, which holds four cases of wine, is partially assembled before shipping to simplify set-up. The header, offered separately, emphasizes food that goes with wine. Recipe pads are attached to the header. Bronze OMA 1983.

ADVERTISER: Ernest & Julio Gallo Winery
Ken Reich, Designer
PRODUCER: Western Tri Pack Corporation

Gallo was looking for an upscale display to conform with the upscale image of its wine products. The result of the search was this permanent wine rack of wood and wire. It ships flat and assembles easily. Holding 36 bottles of wine in the minimum of floor space, the unit can provide message changes as the product or the promotion theme changes. Bronze OMA 1983.

ADVERTISER: Summit Wine Geyser Peak Winery
John Senkovich, President
Robert Platt, Market Analyst
PRODUCER: Mead Merchandising

Introducing a new concept in wine packaging, this carton/dispenser was designed to be placed at the check-out counter. The can in a glass concept tied in the new idea with the familiar concept. Moisture-proof adhesives are used so the carton may be placed in a glass cooler or in cold vaults. Gold OMA 1983.

ADVERTISER: Sunkist Soft Drinks Inc.
Cuyler Caldwell, Director of Sales Promotion
PRODUCER: Dynagraphic Merchandising Corp.

A real inflatable ring is the eye-catcher in this pole display that offers the tube to customers. The full-color lithograph of the young woman was mounted to chipboard and die-cut in shape. Bronze OMA 1983.

ADVERTISER: Dr. Pepper Co.
John Palumba, Director of Merchandise Services
PRODUCER: Thomas A. Schutz Co.

The assymetric design of these clocks seems to attract the eye for longer periods. To keep charges down, the frame was molded in quarters and fastened together mechanically; reducing the size and simplifying plating. Bronze OMA 1983.

ADVERTISER: Pepsico
Al Falvey; Tom Morrison
PRODUCER: Dyment Co.
Mike Kerth, Designer

The shopper can't help reaching for this six-pack as it tips forward off the shelf, but it is in no danger of falling. A battery-operated arm is the secret behind this attention-getter. Best of Show Award, 1983.

ADVERTISER: Dr. Pepper
Charles Cargil
PRODUCER: Ridan Displays
John Gross, Designer

This unit can serve either as a clock or a perpetual calendar, as well as a pencil tray for use at or near the cash register.

ADVERTISER: Pepsico
Al Falvey; Tom Morrison
PRODUCER: Dyment Co.
Mike Kerth, Designer

The ever-pouring can of Pepsi is a sure attention-getter in
supermarkets. Its secret is a spiral cola-colored rod, rotated by a
battery-controlled motor. The battery has a 15-week life. Bronze
OMA 1983.

ADVERTISER: Coca-Cola USA
Richard E. Young, Manager, Point-of-Purchase
PRODUCER: Ridan Displays Inc.
John Gross, Designer

This clock comes in either a red or a white frame, depending on the store decor. An expensive ABS plastic, instead of styrene, gives it the desired wet look. The vertical positioning of the name, and the omission of the full name, "Coca-Cola", also represents an innovation for the company. Bronze OMA 1983.

ADVERTISER: Coca Cola Canada Ltd.
Steve Phillips, Group Product Manager
PRODUCER: CDA Industries Inc.

This illuminated menu sign is versatile and easily up-dated with graphics.

ADVERTISER: Hires, Crush Canada Inc.
Vaughan Wyche, Brand Manager
PRODUCER: CDA Industries Inc.

Provides an appealing, distinct fountain-head dispenser. Its classic and authentic appearance makes it a welcome decorative addition to any outlet.

ADVERTISER: Coca-Cola USA
Richard E. Young, Manager, Point-of-Purchase
PRODUCER: Ridan Displays Inc.
John Gross, Designer

The frames of grass cloth helped to make this the company's most successful non-illuminated menu program.

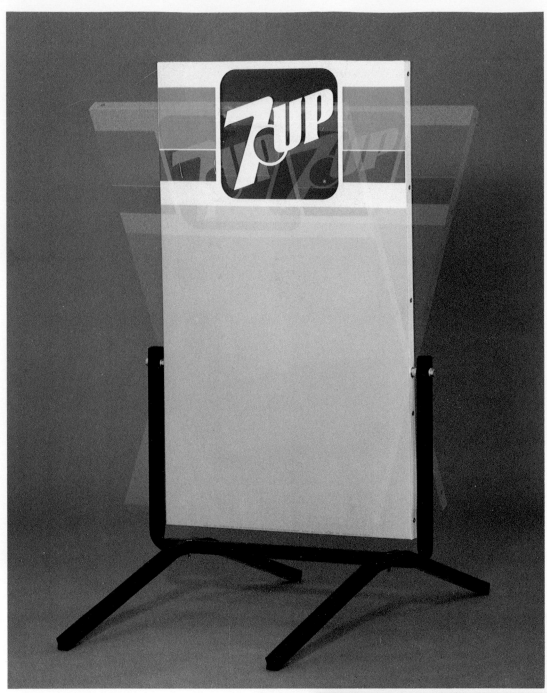

ADVERTISER: The Seven Up Co.
PRODUCER: Stout Industries Inc.

This unit, with its unique below-center pivot and counter weight, will remain stable at wind speeds of up to 100 mph, according to tests. The face can carry lanced pockets or rails for price or message application.

ADVERTISER: The Seven-Up Company, Phillip Morris Co.
Tim Battles, National Retail Sales Director
Paul Rullo, National Retail Sales Manager/Convenience Stores
PRODUCER: Visual Marketing Inc.
John F. Deffner, Designer

Designed to organize soft drink coolers and to encourage impulse
sales, the system consists of two units, a two-tiered server for
small cans and bottles and a single level unit for large bottles. Both
use gravity to keep the product towards the front of the rack. Bronze
OMA 1983.

This elegant pole-topper, with its die-cut dimensional letters in gold foil, captured consumer attention. Not related directly to the Christmas season, the display could be used for other gift occasions. Silver OMA 1983.

ADVERTISER: Old Grand Dad, National Distillers Products Co.
Bob Mutschler, Sales Promotion Manager
Bob Kirschner, Control States Promotion Manager
PRODUCER: American Sign and Marketing Services

The pedestal design makes this unit attach easily to cash register tops, where the down-lighting feature illuminates the register keys in normally low-lit lounges and pubs. Bronze OMA 1983.

ADVERTISER: Johnnie Walker Red, Somerset Importers Ltd.
R. Van Gelderen
PRODUCER: Jerry Moss Inc.
R. Alley, Designer

When calling the toll-free number promoted on the case header, contest entrants will hear the voice of Johnnie Walker giving them the qualifying question they need to complete their entry.

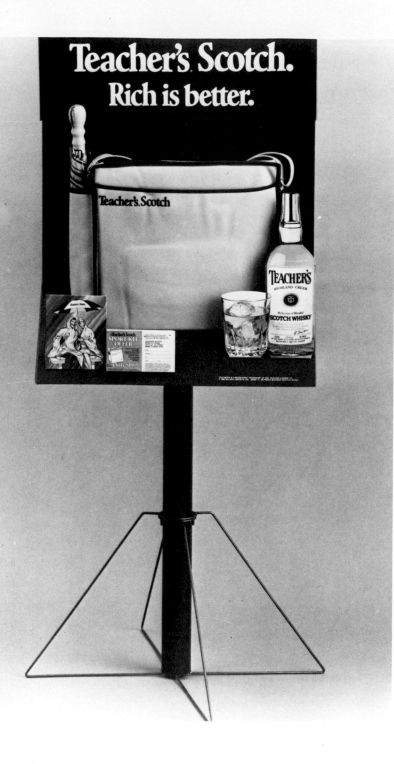

ADVERTISER: Teacher's Scotch, Bacardi Imports Inc.
Elena Batan, Sales Promotion Manager
PRODUCER: P.O.P. Displays Inc.

The premium, a stadium seat with poncho and umbrella, is the highlight of this display. An illustration of the premium in use is next to a pad of order forms. Bronze OMA 1983.

ADVERTISER: Old Bushmills, The Jos. Garneau Co. Brown-Forman Distillers Corp.
Paul C. Field, Sales Promotion Manager
PRODUCER: Wiremasters Inc.
J. M. Scriba Jr., Designer

This compact unit holds four bottles of the product on the check-out counter, which encourages purchase as an add-on. The calendar carries a different sales message of each day. The bottle can be removed from the rear only, thus discouraging pilferage.

ADVERTISER: Hennessy
PRODUCER: Ledan Inc.

This pole display gains attention because of its changing graphics
which alternate between a slogan and an interpretation of it.

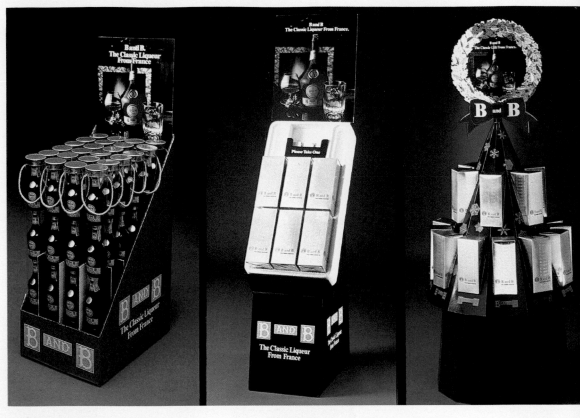

ADVERTISER: B & B, Julius Wile Sons & Co.
Richard C. Bland, President
J.B. Meaders, Advertising & Promotion Director
PRODUCER: Howard/Marlboro Group
Milton Merl, Designer

Three displays that encourage gift purchases of a classic liqueur were attractive to a wide range of retailers. For the low-cost buyer, the display on the left held 24 clear plastic cylinders, each with four mini-bottles. The center unit was a pre-pack, holding six gift boxes in a molded tray, while the final unit, for higher traffic locations, held 18 gift boxes. Bronze OMA 1983.

ADVERTISER: Barton Brands
Dennis Fitzgerald, Marketing Manager
PRODUCER: Chicago Show Printing Co.
Earl D. Barnett, Designer

To achieve a quality image, this unit was made of wood, which commanded premium floor placement over the usual corrugated displays. The header swings down in back for ease of shipment.

ADVERTISER: J&B Scotch; The Paddington Corp. and The Promotional Agency
Richard Papalian, President, The Promotional Agency
D. James McCue, Director, Sales Promotion, Paddington
PRODUCER: Everbrite Electric Signs Inc.

The perpetual calendar achieves three objectives. First, it offers immediate brand recognition while displaying a current advertising graphic. Second, it tells the day and date. Third, it encourages the purchase of the product. The changeable information is printed on spring-rolled Mylar tapes, for easy up-dating. Bronze OMA 1983.

ADVERTISER: Inver House (Fleischmann Distilling Co.)
Mort Mazor, VP, Director of Merchandising
PRODUCER: Howard/Marlboro Group

This prestigious cut-case card stands 20 in. high, and displays the actual premium—a home bar mirror—which can be obtained by the consumer. A pad of coupons bearing the offer is attached.

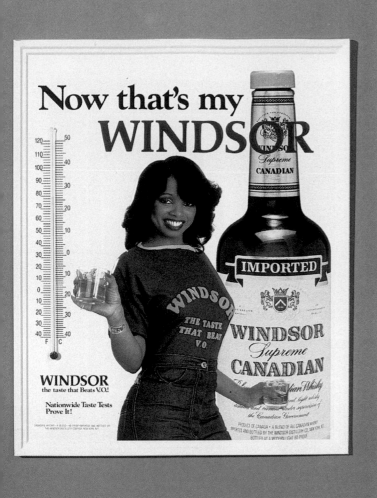

ADVERTISER: Windsor Canadian, National Distillers Products Co.
Jim Ronayne, Sales Promotion Manager, Windsor Canadian
PRODUCER: Stout Industries Inc.

Aimed at the ethnic market, this unit had to be versatile to be acceptable to as many outlets as possible. Screen-printed on aluminum, it can be used outdoors as well as indoors. While usually attached to a wall, it can be slid over the edge of an open case with cardboard tabs and slotted wooden sticks.

ADVERTISER: Various
PRODUCER: Mechanical Mirror Works

The ability of a mirror to make a room seem larger, brighter, or more active makes mirrors etched with messages useful as a display medium, either by itself, as in these examples, or as an element in a larger promotional piece.

...Successful Promotions from Mechanical Mirror

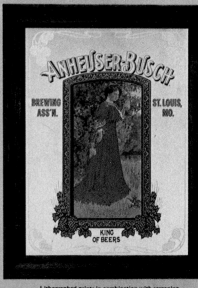

Ornate Framed Mirrors

Lithographed prints in combination with screening and a simulated gold etch with a 2½" wood frame.

Serving Trays — which can even be personalized.

Cast brass frame with logo in simulated etch "Sparkletone" process.

ADVERTISER: Early Times, Brown-Forman Distillers Corp.
Art Peer, Sales Promotion Manager
Cheryl Suhr, Brand Manager
PRODUCER: PW Inc.

To maintain continuing loyalty when a new label was introduced, this display shows the old and the new packages side by side, over a mass display of the product. Bronze OMA 1983.

ADVERTISER: Southern Comfort, Brown-Forman Distillers Corp.
Gail Smiley, Sales Promotion Manager
Robert Hausladen, Associate Brand Manager
PRODUCER: PW Inc.

The oak frame holds a slate chalkboard which can be used by the customer to announce daily features and other special offers, or to hold colorful promotional posters. Bronze OMA 1983.

ADVERTISER: Jack Daniels Distillery
William Hanlan, VP, Advertising
John Beach, Advertising Manager
PRODUCER: Stout Industries Inc.

The old-fashioned sign pole can stand alone or serve as an effective center for case stacking. Four panels, silkscreened of aluminum sheet, are made available to meet varying situations. These panels can also be mounted on the wall or as free-standing displays, using a cardboard easel. Silver OMA 1983.

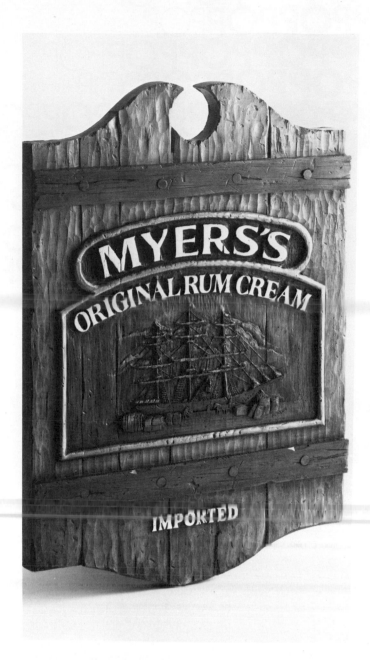

ADVERTISER: Myers's Original Rum Cream, Joseph E. Seagram & Sons Inc.
Thomas McInerney, VP, Marketing
Jonathan Giesberg, Product Manager
PRODUCER: Foam Visions Inc.
Siebel/Mohr, Designer

This plaque, of molded polystyrene, contributes a traditional
nautical feeling to a new product. A multi-colored finish was
achieved through masking and hand-painting. Bronze OMA 1983.

ADVERTISER: Remy Martin, Premiere Wine Merchants Inc.
Stan Schneiderman, Sales Promotion Manager
PRODUCER: Elite Marketing Ltd.
Ray Sternbergh, Designer

An elegant display for an elegant product. The inner cylinder,
lithographed in four colors and varnished, turned within a clear
plastic cylinder, silk-screened in two horizontal bands, from the
inside. Bronze OMA 1983.

POPPOPPOPPOP
PPOPPOPPOPPOP
POPPOPPOPPOP
POPPOPPOPPOPPOP
POPPOPPOPPOP
POPPOPPOPPOPF
POPPOPPOPPO
POPPOPPOPP
POPPOPPOPPO

8

Personal Products and Accessories

A wide variety of products are included in this chapter, and as a result, a wide variety of point-of-purchase displays, ranging from the simple and straightforward product organizer, to the high fashion approach of quality jewelry. It includes impulse items like children's toys and articles bought with more serious consideration, like fine cameras. In this category are everyday articles like pantyhose and special-purpose ones like ski boots.

Therefore, within this single chapter can be found examples of displays designed to do each of the tasks outlined earlier as an objective of p.o.p.

One of the specific objectives that can be accomplished by a point-of-purchase display is the organization of a line of products, especially where the profit margin is low and the individual sale does not always support the investment of the time of a salesperson. A good p.o.p. unit can help the customer to find, without the aid of a salesclerk, exactly which item he wants. There are some good examples of this in the sub-category of Office Equipment and Supplies.

Another objective of point-of-purchase advertising is to encourage impulse sales, to display the product in such a fashion

that it is easy to find and to select. Toys, books, and games, included in this chapter, have displays that fall in this group.

Other displays are designed to explain a product to the customer, to point out its unique characteristics, to distinguish one brand from another, and to help the consumer logically move closer to the buying decision. This becomes more important as it becomes more difficult, in many kinds of stores, to have salespeople who are knowledgeable about all the products carried in stock. Displays for photographic equipment often fall in this group.

Other products need to be presented in such a way that the customer can easily find the color or the style he or she wants. Here there is a need to displaying many items at once, allowing the prospect to make his selection rapidly. Such disparate items as sunglasses and greeting cards fall in this group, and displays designed for this purpose are illustrated in this chapter.

Retailers like to make it both possible and easy for the customer to pick up and handle a product. They know that moving the product from the shelf or the counter into the hand increases the probability of the purchase. They know also that, unfortunately, it increases the probability of pilferage, and this becomes a major factor with small items like jewelry, or highly

desirable items like electronic gadgets. Well-designed displays can sometimes permit handling while at the same time discouraging pilfering.

Finally, displays can often demonstrate a product or a selling point without the aid of a salesperson. This, too, moves a prospect closer to a sale. A very nice example of this is the display for a waterproof hiking boot, which includes almost all the best features of a p.o.p. display. In the first place, it uses real running water, which draws attention because of both motion and sound. It is attractive, showing the product in its most natural setting. And finally, because the water actually runs over the boot, it demonstrates convincingly the prime benefit of the product.

Throughout this entire book, examples have appeared of displays designed to achieve one or more of these objectives; but no single chapter seems to illustrate as many objectives as does this one.

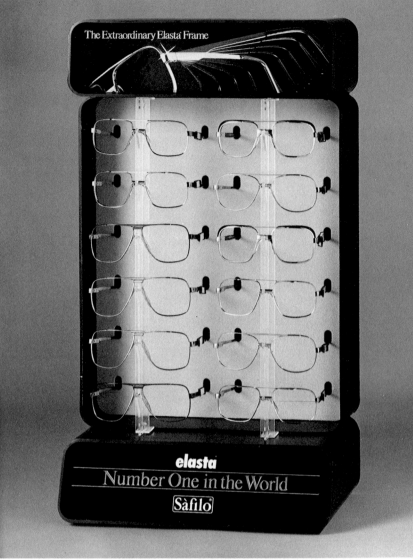

ADVERTISER: Starline Optical
George Rich, President
PRODUCER: Marketing Methods Inc.
Thomas Mulvihill

A rotating stand has three pockets to hold consumer brochures.

ADVERTISER: Elasta Eyewear, Starline Optical
George Rich, President
PRODUCER: Marketing Methods Inc.

This counter display is injection-molded in a single piece, making it one of the largest molded displays produced.

ADVERTISER: Optyl Fashion Eyewear
Nick Scarcella

PRODUCER: Marketing Methods Inc.
Thomas Mulvihill, Designer

Six pairs of fashion frames are displayed under a pilfer resistant cover. Three signs come with this unit, so the retailer can select the line to be featured.

ADVERTISER: Carrera Int.
Nick Scarcella
PRODUCER: Marketing Methods Inc.
Thomas Mulvihill, Designer

This display of ski goggles uses the minimum amount of counter space.

ADVERTISER: Carrera Int.
Rich Sowa
PRODUCER: Marketing Methods Inc.
Thomas Mulvihill, Designer

This stepped counter display holds 12 sun glasses, protected from pilferage, but easily reached, with a convenient mirror. A storage compartment is in the rear.

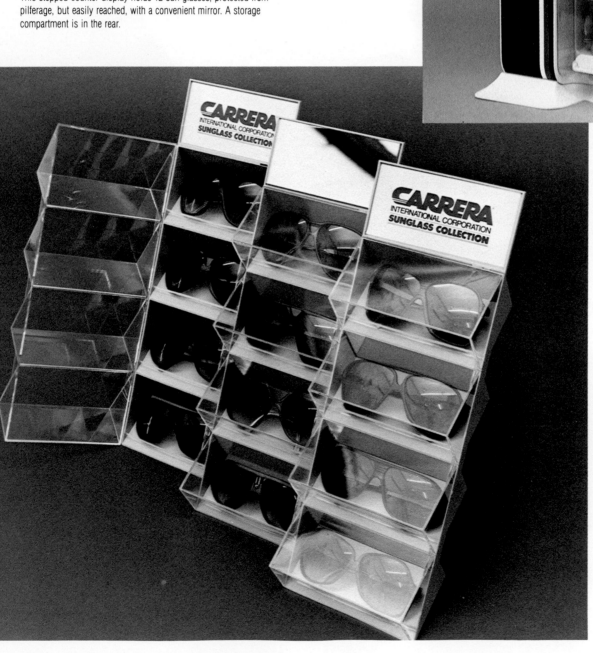

ADVERTISER: Carrera Int.
Rick Sowa
PRODUCER: Marketing Methods Inc.
Thomas Mulvihill, Designer

Six ski goggles are kept in this rotating counter display, which can be made into one that holds 12, simply by adding similar components.

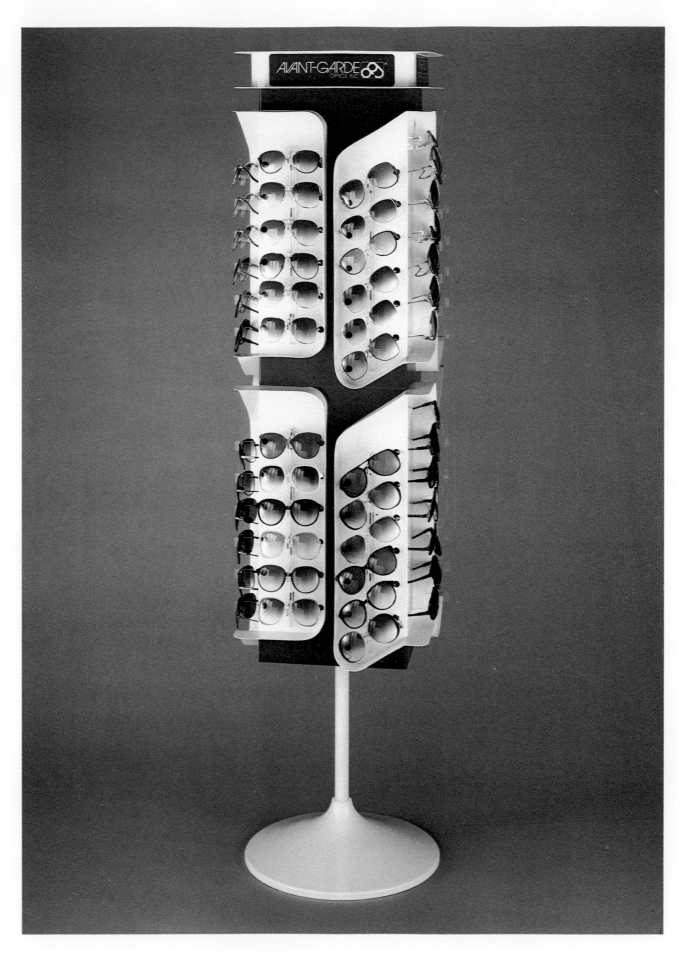

ADVERTISER: Avant-Garde Optics
Jerry Ross
PRODUCER: Marketing Methods Inc.

This display, designed for opticians' and optometrists' offices, holds 96 pair of frames, and rotates easily.

ADVERTISER: Corning Glass Works, Optical Products
Bill Opies

PRODUCER: Einson-Freeman Inc.
Gary Dubcik

Turning a cardboard wheel demonstrates how the lens changes
color according to the light. This simple cardboard unit replaced an
in-store demonstrator that cost about 25 times as much.

ADVERTISER: Bonneau/Sunsensor
Peggy Hines

PRODUCER: Einson-Freeman Inc.
Robin Crebbin

Holding 48 pairs of sun glasses, this rotating floor unit is low
enough in cost to be considered a temporary display.

ADVERTISER: Chameleon, Corning Glass Works
James A. Burt Jr., Merchandising and Promotional Manager
PRODUCER: Thomas A. Schutz Co.

The unusual triangular shape of this free-standing display sets its
tone. The trays use clear plastic for the shelves, to provide
maximum visibility for the glasses, and translucent for the rear
walls to diffuse the fluorescent lamps set in the central column.
Easy access makes it tempting to try on a pair of glasses and look
at one's self in the mirrors set into the side panels. Bronze OMA
1983.

ADVERTISER: Tropic-Cal of Canada Ltd.
Floyd Owen, President
PRODUCER: CDA Industries Inc.

This illuminated sun-glass merchandiser holds 120 pairs of
glasses. The top mirrors can be replaced at the retailer's option.

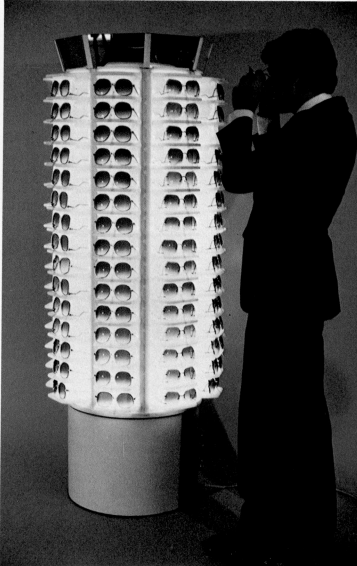

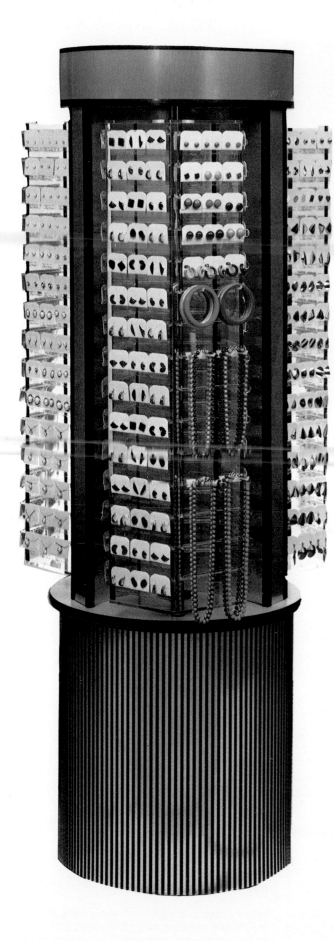

ADVERTISER: Pakula and Co.
Gerry Rapoport, VP, National Accounts
PRODUCER: Displayco East

Pakula, which sells its jewelry in J. C. Penney stores, needed to up-date its displays as Penney up-dated its own look. This unit, only 20 inches wide, is a self-contained, self-service area with a pleasing presentation. The top of the tower rotates, as does each individual tower. Bronze OMA 1983.

ADVERTISER: Generic
PRODUCER: Marketing Methods Inc.

This rotating display, originally designed for Casual Corner Stores, holds 288 earring cards in less than one square foot of counter space.

ADVERTISER: Timex
Geri Allen
PRODUCER: Mechtronics

It's hard to ignore an open and modern-looking display. This unit, less than 20 in. square, and nearly 6 ft. tall, is easy to find room for. The tower of product illuminated by an overhead spot, rotates slowly. When the customer sees a watch he wishes to inspect, he can touch a button to stop the rotation. Bronze OMA 1983.

ADVERTISER: Timex Corporation
Jerri Allen, Display Manager
Maurice Noonan, Buyer
PRODUCER: Display Systems Inc.

This counter display holds 20 watches, all easily examined from the front. The copper of the package was set off with the beige of the display and its gold highlights. The tower permitted an additional model to be featured, and permitted a changeable graphic panel. Two additional panels were included with the unit when it was shipped. The tower could also be used for storage of batteries, additional watches, or a variety of other products.

ADVERTISER: Lorus Canada
Bill Penney
PRODUCER: Gorrie Advertising Services
Paul Whittington, Designer

The component construction permits on the spot customization.

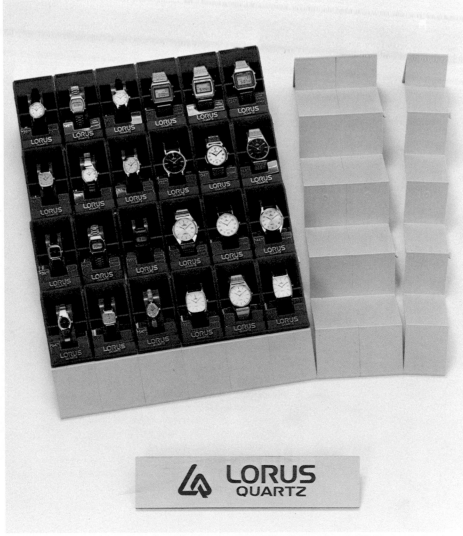

ADVERTISER: Seiko Time Corp.
David Strousse
PRODUCER: Mechtronics Corp.

Each section of this counter display shows the product against a
rear-lit transparency, related to the specific watches shown. The unit
can be rotated by hand to view the other watches on display, or to
read the copy, printed on panels next to the watches. Bronze OMA
1983.

ADVERTISER: Bic Pen Corp.
Ray Alonso, Marketing Services Manager
PRODUCER: Henschel-Steinau Inc.

Designed especially for Walgreen and Rite Aid stores, this
merchandiser had to carry products from three lighter
manufacturers. Of the four facings for carded merchandise, Bic was
used for two, and one each for Cricket and Scripto. As many as
1,000 carded lighters could be held on the 4 sides, and several
hundred more could be held in the dump bin below. Bronze OMA
1983.

ADVERTISER: Zippo Manufacturing Co.
William W. Jones

PRODUCER: Zippo Manufacturing Co.

This attractive counter display uses both light and motion to attract attention. The light in the canopy not only shines on the slanted lighters, taking advantage of the polished metal surfaces, but it illuminates the plastic trademark in the header. Slow rotation allows the customer to view all the lighters easily. The retailer can display any combination of styles he wishes, and the clear plastic case prevents pilferage.

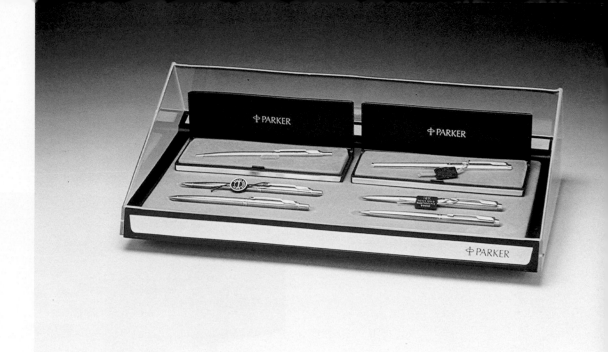

ADVERTISER: Parker Pen Co.
Paula Falk, Marketing Materials Manager
PRODUCER: Benchmarc Display Inc.

Since many retailers who handle the product object to manufacturers' displays, this unit was designed to be compatible with all store decors, and be aesthetically pleasing. This was achieved by a clean, contemporary design, with a clear cover that makes the product the eye-catcher, yet protects it against pilferage.

ADVERTISER: A.T. Cross Co.
Michael Drolet, Merchandising Manager
PRODUCER: Marketing Methods Inc.
Thomas Mulvihill, Designer

To suggest buying a pen and pencil set as a gift, the product is placed in this unit of clear and black styrene, embellished with a ribbon and artificial flowers, and a card which reminds the viewer of a gift-giving occasion. The card can be changed to keep the display current. Bronze OMA 1983.

ADVERTISER: Scripto Inc.
　　　　　　　Ken Bogle
PRODUCER: Patrick H. Joyce & Associates

This counter-top display always looks full, since it positions pencils
to the front when loading.

ADVERTISER: Parker Pen Co.
　　　　　　　Paula Frank, Marketing Materials Manager
PRODUCER: Benchmarc Display Inc.
　　　　　　　Edwin Miller, Designer

The unit displays four gift sets, and ships with an additional seven
units packed in. It is compact, pilfer-resistant, and fits the outlets.
Many dealers removed the header after the promotional period, and
kept the display as a permanent unit. Bronze OMA 1983.

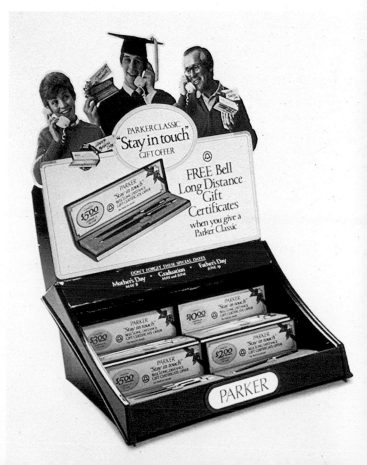

This unit, which can sit on a counter top or be mounted to a wall, holds more than 100 templates. The peg hooks are adjustable to permit the retailer to display the products in any order or selection he wants.

Using a cartridge for replacement lead is a new concept in mechanical pencils, and Berol wanted to make sure the consumer knew about it. This counter-top display attracted attention with a larger-than-life photo of the cartridges. Bronze OMA 1983.

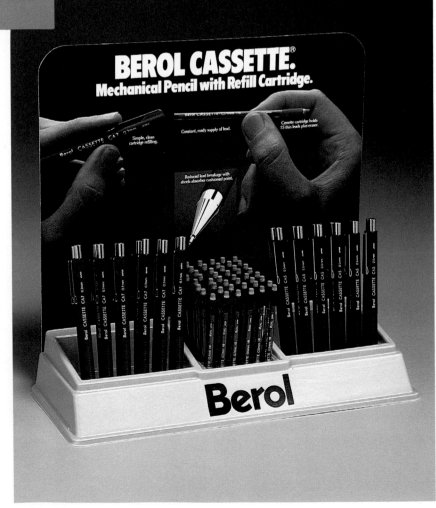

ADVERTISER: Sheaffer Eaton
PRODUCER: Thomson-Leeds Co. Inc.

A complete line of business-oriented notebooks can be shown in this injection-molded display. The full-color, lithoed riser simply slips into the back of the display. Plastic dividers are adjustable for any desired assortment.

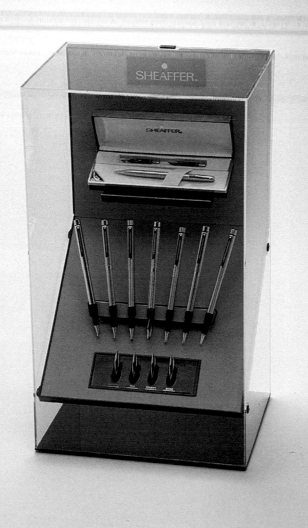

ADVERTISER: Sheaffer Eaton
ADVERTISER: Thomson-Leeds Co. Inc.

The client wanted to bring its fine writing instruments one step closer to the consumer, and this counter-top display was the means. Housed in clear acrylic, the pens, mounted at a writing angle, could be seen from many angles, but a lock on the back made it pilfer-resistant. The classic design earned it placement in many stores that do not normally use advertiser-supplied displays.

ADVERTISER: Cardinal Products, Josten's Business Products Inc.
John Young, Director of Marketing and Sales
PRODUCER: Visual Marketing
Lawrence J. Zock, Designer

Rotating 360 degrees, this floor display of vinyl clad chipboard and hardboard, makes self-selection easy. Bronze OMA 1982.

ADVERTISER: Sanford Ink
Ron Bielke
PRODUCER: Patrick H. Joyce & Associates
Hal Nickel, Designer

This metal and particle board structure holds over $2000 worth of merchandise, and is self-contained, including informative price tags, selection charts, a doodle pad, and even a stock storage compartment with a roll-up door.

ADVERTISER: Duncan Enterprise
Richard Huddleson, Director of Advertising

PRODUCER: Continental Graphics
Colin Bedding, Design Director

Designed for ceramic supply stores, this unit was used to introduce a line of very fine and expensive specialty brushes. The brushes do not need to be removed from the display to see their characteristics.

ADVERTISER: Generic
PRODUCER: Deijon Inc.

This rotating display can be used for magazines and soft cover books. It is adjustable to varying publications, and manages to let most of the cover be visible.

ADVERTISER: Generic
PRODUCER: Deijon Inc.

This patented display, called Booktique, can be produced to hold material of various sizes, but in all its variations, shows the complete front covers and spines of the items it is displaying.

ADVERTISER: Time Life Books
PRODUCER: Deijon Inc.

Three rotating racks within a rotating display permit both the front and back of the books to be seen, especially valuable with a line as colorful as this.

ADVERTISER: Walden/Silhouette
PRODUCER: Deijon Inc.

This unit, with its rotating racks, has a high capacity for paperback books, and is designed to stand at the end of a double shelf display unit.

ADVERTISER: Generic
PRODUCER: Deijon Inc.

This self-standing unit, made of metal tubing and wire, is designed to hold impulse items, like chewing gum and magazines, in a high-impulse area near the check-out counters of a supermarket.

ADVERTISER: Walden Book Stores
Ron Jaffe
PRODUCER: Deijon Inc.
Vincent Gambello, Designer

Designed to put children's books within the reach of children, this
rotating stand handles books of varying sizes.

ADVERTISER: B. Dalton Bookstores
PRODUCER: Deijon Inc.
Vince Gambello, Designer

This permanent display maximizes and organizes the product showings, making it easy for customers to browse and select titles. Its mass impact encourages add-on sales.

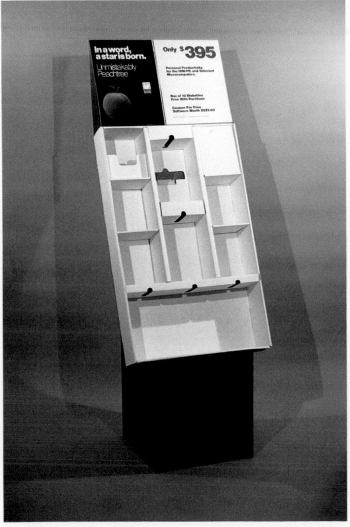

ADVERTISER: Peachtree Software, Wabash Data Tech Inc.
Alan Whitebread, Marketing Manager, Diskettes
PRODUCER: Acorn Display

Wabash needed a display that presented computer software and diskettes in a fast-paced, high-growth computer market. Full-color lithography on the riser permitted continuity with the package, while the main rack was of unprinted corrugated, divided into bins to take varied product cartons. Bronze OMA 1983.

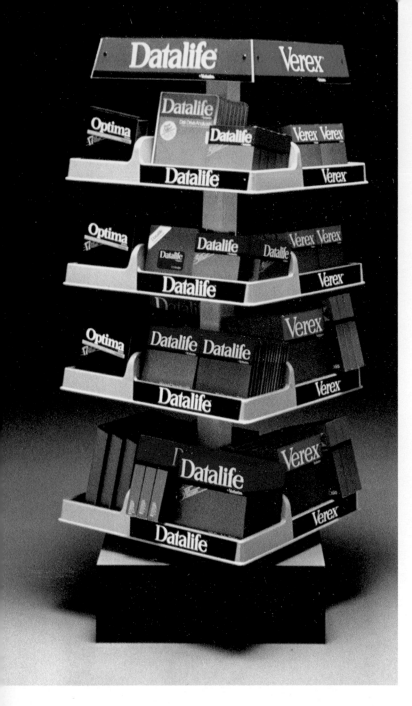

ADVERTISER: Verbatim Corporation
Rod Crisp, Corporate Marketing Director
Earl Liebich, Distribution Marketing Manager
PRODUCER: Deijon Inc.

With four shelves and 16 pockets, this rotating display holds more than 150 packages in a space only two feet square. The tray and header signs can be changed easily to assign the space according to local needs. Bronze OMA 1983

ADVERTISER: TDK Electronics Corp.
PRODUCER: Displayonix Corporation

This permanent merchandiser moved the product from store shelves to the point-of-sale. Standing only 32 in. high, and using only 1.5 sq. ft. of counter space, it holds 60 videotape packages.

ADVERTISER: Memorex International Ltd.
Rolf Christopherson, Manager, Flexible Discs
PRODUCER: Dauman Displays Inc.

This colorful display, using the package colors, enhances brand recognition, and helps the dealer organize his presentation, making customer selection easier. Bronze OMA 1983. 1st prize, Assn. of Point of Sale Advertising, London, 1983.

ADVERTISER: Generic
PRODUCER: Deijon Inc.

This patented display, called Booktique, can be produced to hold material of various sizes, but in all its variations, shows the complete front covers and spines of the items it is displaying.

ADVERTISER: Maxell Corp. of America
Carl Lindquist
PRODUCER: Rob Robinson Marketing Inc.
Dan Robinson, Designer

This stand of chrome tubing, and clear plastic, can be shipped, yet assembles easily. It holds an assortment of products, both on shelves, and hanging from hooks.

ADVERTISER: Fuji Film
PRODUCER: Flite Marketing Ltd.
Ray Sternbergh, Designer

This unit combines injection molding, extrusions, and silk screen. It contains a full line of the product, and assures rotation of the stock, since film is withdrawn from the bottom, but inserted from the top. It can stand on a counter or be mounted on the wall.

ADVERTISER: Xerox Corp.
Terry Mazlarz
PRODUCER: Einson Freeman Inc.
Gary Bobcik, Designer

This unit provided computer retailers with the industry's first self-contained, free-standing, multi-media selling center. A flip chart takes the prospect through the operations of the equipment without the presence of a salesman.

ADVERTISER: Commodore Business Machines Ltd.
James Copland, National Sales Manager, Consumer Division
PRODUCER: CDA Industries

This space-saving, columnar unit holds a large supply of inventory, with plenty of space for a sales message. The graphics can easily be changed to update the display.

ADVERTISER: IBM
Curt Hoopingarner
PRODUCER: Patrick H. Joyce & Associates
Hal Nickel, Designer

This counter merchandiser, with its high tech, quality look, displays a varied assortment of typewriter elements, protected against pilferage. Back-up stock can be stored in the rear of the unit.

ADVERTISER: H.D. Lee Company
Georgia Kelly, Cooperative Advertising Coordinator
PRODUCER: E. and E. Specialties
Nelson Orwig

This colorful sign, lithographed on plastic, because of its light weight can be affixed easily to walls. It is a more-or-less permanent fixture, since new graphics can quickly be installed in the frame. Gold OMA 1981.

ADVERTISER: Wrangler, Blue Bell Inc.
Clayton Ramsey
PRODUCER: Wiremasters Inc.
J. M. Scriba Jr., Designer

To overcome the problem of selling jeans in stores without dressing rooms, this portable dressing room, 39 × 27 in. was developed. On the outside it holds as many as 28 trays, with a plastic channel on each to carry a sign giving size, price, and stock numbers. Bronze OMA 1982.

ADVERTISER: Maverick Jeans Wear
Wayne Hodges, Director of Marketing
PRODUCER: Trans World Mfg. Corp.

An effort to get the product sold in food and drug stores guided the design of this floor stand. The boxed jeans were arranged by size, with sizing information on the shelf rails. The pair of jeans suspended from the display allowed for consumer inspection without opening up the boxes. Bronze OMA 1983.

ADVERTISER: Hanson Ski Boots, Daiwa Sports Inc.
William R. Perry, VP and General Manager
PRODUCER: DCI Marketing

The high-tech design of the boot is reflected in the sleekness of this two-part display. The upper section can stand by itself on a counter, or can be placed on a matching free-standing base.

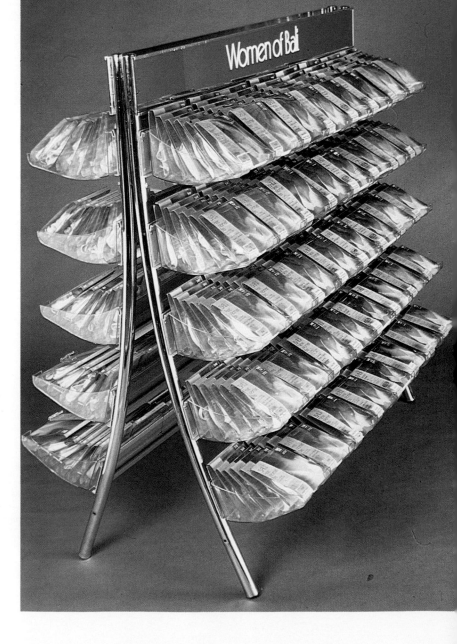

ADVERTISER: Bali Company
Steve Marcus, General Manager and Chief Operating Officer
PRODUCER: The Howard/Marlboro Group
Howard Nathan, Designer

The clear plastic trays, five on each side of this unit, can each hold four dozen packages. The curved legs not only add stability to the display, but increase the visibility of the lower shelves.

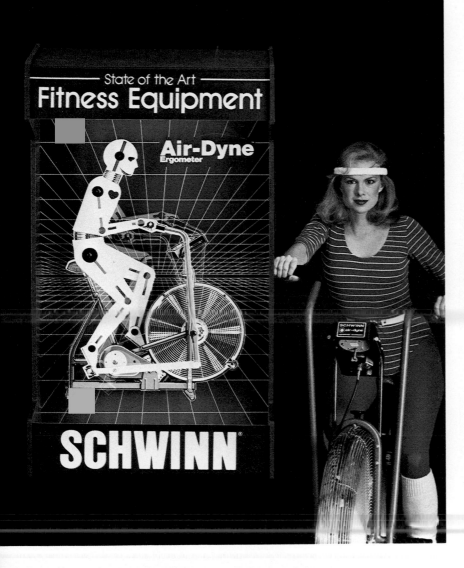

ADVERTISER: Excelsior Fitness Equipment Co. A. Schwinn Co.
Al Fritz, President
Gerry O'Keefe, VP, Marketing
PRODUCER: Thomas A. Schutz Co.

This floor display stops traffic with its motion. The futuristic man moves his feet and legs, rocking back and forth as he would do on an actual machine. As he pedals, the wheel turns. The lit display can serve as a night light, adding hours to the impact of the unit. Gold OMA 1983.

ADVERTISER: Spalding, Div. of Questor Corp.
Al Bender, Marketing Director
Chuck Yash, Marketing Director
PRODUCER: Henschel-Steinau Inc.

This unit turns the name of the product into an eye catching, traffic-stopping display. The presentation makes it simple for the prospect to pick up and swing one of the clubs on display. Bronze OMA 1983.

ADVERTISER: American Hosiery Corp.
Manuel Oliveira, President
PRODUCER: ABCO Wire and Metal Products
Walter Risher Sr., Designer

This permanent display holds 30 columns of the product, each face unobscured. Stock is kept at the front of the rack through gravity. The use of plastic at the front of each row of racks and on the sides increases the visibility of the product. Bronze OMA 1983.

ADVERTISER: Parke-Davis division, Warner Lambert Inc.
Larry Haverkost, Senior Product Manager
George B. Cavic, Product Manager
PRODUCER: Johnstons & Associates Inc.
Bert Cain, Designer

Soft line and elegant style give this compact display a department store look and a winning personality. The tray system solves a crucial problem by securely displaying full facings of packages in an upright position. The shelf labels can easily be changed to proportion the product types according to demand, and the header can be replaced for special promotions. Bronze OMA 1983.

ADVERTISER: Leverenz Shoe Co.
Susan Peterson, Advertising Manager
PRODUCER: Process Displays Inc.

The use of wood-textured materials gives this sign, display and accessory a feeling of old-world flavor and quality. Bronze OMA 1983.

ADVERTISER: The Timberland Co.
Stanley Kravitz, Executive VP
LouAnn Santin, Director, Marketing Services
PRODUCER: DCI Marketing

There's nothing better than an actual demonstration to prove a point, and here's an excellent example. To demonstrate that the boot is waterproof, the toe is constantly covered by flowing water, circulated by a built-in pump. The customer can reach into the inside of the boot to see for himself how dry the inside has been kept.

ADVERTISER: Leverenz Shoe Co.
Susan Peterson, Advertising Manager
PRODUCER: Process Displays Inc.

The use of wood-textured materials gives this group of signs, displays and other accessories a feeling of old-world flavor and quality. Bronze OMA 1983.

ADVERTISER: Argus Communications
James Porst, Vice President
Michael Hayes, Merchandising Manager
PRODUCER: E. and E. Specialties, Nelson Orwig, Designer

With this display, the customer can browse through the assortment to find a favorite, without damage to the stock. This permits the header to feature the star character of the series. Bronze OMA 1983.

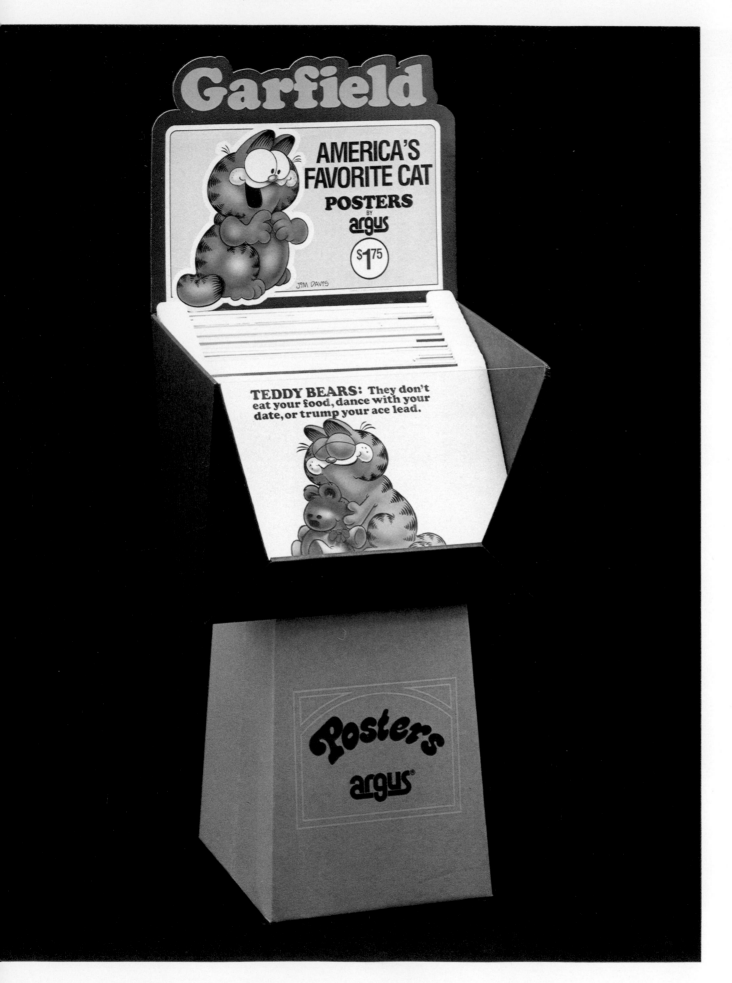

ADVERTISER: Playskool Inc.
George Snyder, Advertising Manager

PRODUCER: Acorn Display

This compact display ships flat and sets up easily, can stand on a counter-top or fit on a gondola shelf. The unit holds the puzzles on steps, so the identification strip on the top of each puzzle is easily seen. Bronze OMA 1983.

ADVERTISER: Argus Communications
James Porst, Vice President
Michael Hayes, Merchandising Manager

PRODUCER: E. and E. Specialties, Nelson Orwig, Designer

The specially-designed, vacuum-formed trays stack for shipping and storing, resulting in substantial savings. It's easy to assemble and to keep clean. It permits an unobstructed view of 56 different postcards. The rotation helps make it very shoppable and easy to place. Bronze OMA 1983.

ADVERTISER: Hershey Foods Corp.
Rick M. Rocchi, Manager, Special Business
Paul D. Hoch, Manager
PRODUCER: Miller Manufacturing Co.

This solid maplewood piece, with four mirrored shelves, ties in with the nostalgic nature of the Hershey-related gifts. Bronze OMA 1983.

ADVERTISER: Cole
Bobbie Sommer
PRODUCER: Creative Displays Inc.
Bob Sparkowski, Designer

This pillar display seems to be reaching out to the passerby, offering him a key ring.

ADVERTISER: American Greetings
Gary Beck, Creative Marketing Services
PRODUCER: Creative Displays Inc.
Phil Sera, Designer

A nostalgic feeling is engendered by this display, simulating a pet shop window.

ADVERTISER: Applause, Knickerbocker Toy Co.
Leslie Gross, Merchandising Manager
PRODUCER: Design Productions

This four tiered tower, which holds the unboxed dolls by a simple cord, make it easy for the customer to see, touch, and buy a doll from this display. Bronze OMA 1983.

ADVERTISER: Texas Instruments Inc.
Roland E. Kalmbach, POP Exhibits Manager
PRODUCER: DCI Marketing

This unit brings the product out of counter and wall cases and puts it where both adults and children can have hands-on access. This, in turn, leads to sales. The upper section can stand on a counter or gondola. The units are unobtrusively clamped to the back wall. They are plugged into a built-in electrical system, so they are ready to work. A base section that holds additional product turns it into a free-standing unit. Bronze OMA 1983.

ADVERTISER: Hallmark Cards Inc.
Robert Owen, Senior Fixture Designer
David Mowatzke, Design Supervisor
PRODUCER: Eddy Associates Inc.

The growing hobby of collecting and using stickers demanded a way in which customers could quickly see what was available. This floor display achieved its purpose by including four rotating islands, each capable of holding 40 peg mounted sticker cards.

ADVERTISER: Bucilla, Armour Handcrafts
Nancy Setter
PRODUCER: Marketing Methods Inc.
Dan Antognini, Designer

This display can be set up as illustrated, or back-to-back in half the space.

ADVERTISER: Hallmark Cards Inc.
Robert Owen, Senior Fixture Designer
David Nowatzke, Design Supervisor
PRODUCER: Eddy Associates Inc.

Handling refills for phone books, photo albums, etc, has always been bothersome in retail stores, but this stackable merchandiser has removed many of the headaches. The labels and the easy pull handle turns it into a self-service operation which frees up store personnel's valuable time. Bronze OMA 1983.

ADVERTISER: Hennegan
Bill Charles
PRODUCER: The Dyment Co.
Tom Riga, Designer

This display was intended to be used as part of a promotion for children. Die-cut, embossed, and mounted at various distances from the background, the display serves as a backdrop for taking pictures of children, who can step behind the basket, so they appear to be in the balloon.

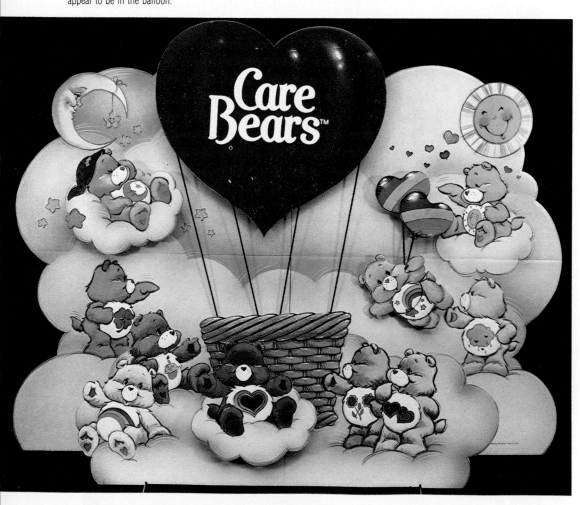

ADVERTISER: Smurfette, Wallace Berrie & Co. Inc.
Bob Calabrese, VP, Production
Gary Trumbo, VP, Marketing
PRODUCER: Harbor Industries Inc.

Adjustable shelves permit the retailer to select which products to highlight. Castors are used below the base so that the unit can be easily placed and relocated. It can be used free-standing, as a gondola, or as a cap display. Bronze OMA 1983.

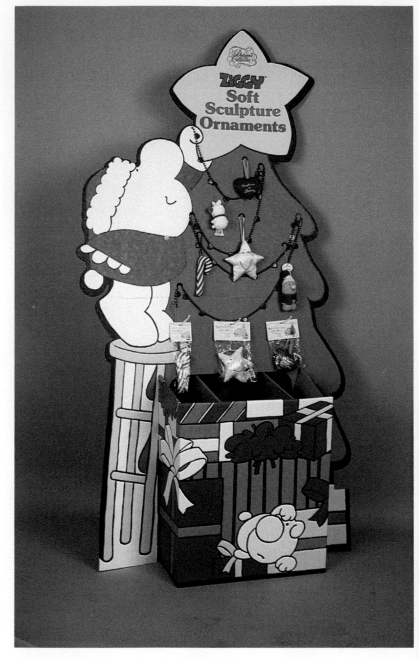

ADVERTISER: Hallmark Cards Inc.
Edward L. Grant, Creative Design Manager
PRODUCER: E. and E. Specialties
Roger White, Designer

This Christmas tree display of holiday greetings sets up rapidly, opening much like an umbrella, so it can be shipped. Bronze OMA 1976.

ADVERTISER: American Greetings
Gary Beck, Creative Marketing Services
PRODUCER: Creative Displays
John Pettibone, Designer

The product is shown in this dump bin display for soft ornaments.

ADVERTISER: American Greetings Corp.
Charlie Wexstaff, Senior Industrial Designer
Ed Gandolf, Manager of Design Engineering
PRODUCER: A.G. Industries

One of a series of in-store signs designed to introduce and
emphasize a new corporate logo, it achieves a high-tech image with
new materials and manufacturing processes. Bronze OMA 1983.

ADVERTISER: Drawing Board Greeting Cards
Barry Yancey, Merchandising Manager
PRODUCER: Acorn Display

The simple design of this corrugated unit allows the cards on
display to be the main attraction. The cards are held straight up, in
ten rows. The header can be replaced or covered to extend the life
of this unit into other seasons. Bronze OMA 1983.

ADVERTISER: Tomy Corporation
William Carlson, Executive VP, Marketing and Sales
Barbara Schwecke, Advertising Manager
PRODUCER: DCI Marketing

This counter unit, with its three-dimensional header, attracts attention to the working demonstration model on the unit base. The customer can pick up the game and actually play it, but an unobtrusive steel cable keeps it firmly attached to the display. Bronze OMA 1983.

ADVERTISER: Random House Inc.
Sylvia Bloomberg, Director, Trade Promotion
PRODUCER: Container Corporation of America

This display is all black, to tie in with the black-clad Darth Vader. It holds 16 facings of 12 bookmarks each, featuring different characters from the Star Wars films.

ADVERTISER: Mattel Toys
Marty Gelfand
PRODUCER: Patrick H. Joyce & Associates

Interchangeable headers permit the retailer to keep the unit fresh and active by using it to promote different product lines, while maintaining the impact of the Mattel name.

POPPOPPOPPOPPOP
POPPOPPOPPOPPOP
POPPOPPOPPOPPOP
POPPOPPOPPOPPOP
POPPOPPOPPOPPOP
POPPOPPOPPOPPOP
POPPOPPOPPOPPOP
POPPOPPOPPOPPOP
POPPOPPOPPOPP
POPPOPPOPPOP

9

Services

The broad category of services, which includes industries as widely different as insurance brokers and hamburger restaurants, is not a heavy user of point-of-purchase advertising. The thinness of this chapter is not a reflection of the attitude of the author, but rather the result of the paucity of submissions that could be assigned to this group.

In the first place, professional services do little advertising, of any kind, and their use of p.o.p. reflects this attitude. Insurance companies often prepare p.o.p. displays for use by their independent agents, including illuminated office clocks, decals for windows, and so on. Even plaques awarded for achievements in sales or administration—and many are awarded—are a form of point-of-purchase advertising. But little emphasis is placed on this promotion, and the objective is often more to build goodwill among agents than to promote sales directly to the customer.

The fast food restaurant category is quite different, however. There is active competition among the various franchise systems, and advertising, especially on

television, is a heavy tool. The objective, of course, is to build patronage, to persuade the hungry prospect to select establishment A rather than establishment B. Point-of-purchase meets this need through identification signs. Most familiar, perhaps, are the golden arches of McDonald's. The sign and architecture of each of the chains acts as a magnet, reinforcing the image of the restaurant and making it easy for the prospect to find the desired place.

Once the customer has walked into the restaurant, point-of-purchase plays a different role. There is no longer any question of whether a purchase will or will not be made, but rather of what will be bought. The printed menu has been replaced, in these food service establishments, by the large reader board, usually placed immediately over the order counter—a form of point-of-purchase that has been borrowed from the soft drink and beer industries, long regular users of this device. In addition, p.o.p. can be used to speed up selection from the menu, to encourage the selection of more profitable items from the menu, to introduce new items, and to encourage participation in a promotion, most of which help build brand loyalty and continuity.

In the opinion of a number of people who follow developments in marketing, too high a proportion of promotional funds is assigned to the more glamorous medium of television. While television reaches a large audience, that audience includes many who may have no interest in buying, while p.o.p.'s audience always wants to buy, as evidenced by their presence in the store. John M. Kawula, vice-president of POPAI, pointed out in *Premium/Incentive Business* that a study conducted for the National Live Stock & Meat Board indicated that in-store advertising increased beef movement an average of 16 percent. He points out that the very successful "Where's the beef?" commercial brought great attention to its sponsor, Wendy's, but questions whether its $8 million cost produced that much increased revenue. That amount of promotional money, he adds, would have paid for a year-round p.o.p. program in every restaurant in the chain.

ADVERTISER: Generic
PRODUCER: Einson Freeman

This instant stacker display can be used in a variety of configurations. A compact, hand-held package or a complete display can be assembled almost instantly, and can be folded up again just as quickly.

ADVERTISER: Bally's Park Place Casino Hotel, Atlantic City NJ
Barry Fine, VP, Food & Beverage
PRODUCER: Design Unlimited/Culinary Concepts
Lew Lehrman, designer

This menu folds flat, or can stand on the table like a tent, but when it is opened, three die-cut sundaes stand out from the back panel.

ADVERTISER: Sands Hotel, Atlantic City NJ
Ralph Taylor, VP, Food & Beverage
PRODUCER: Design Unlimited/Culinary Concepts
Lew Lehrman, designer

These two menus are made of die-cut stock, fitted together without glue or fasteners. The luscious color illustrations make it difficult to turn down a dessert.

ADVERTISER: Hardee's
Ted Demmon
PRODUCER: Einson Freeman
Gary Bobcik, Designer

This large display with built-in motion is designed to involve children. It dispenses premiums as an aid in building traffic.

ADVERTISER: Generic
PRODUCER: Einson Freeman

This instant stacker display can be used in a variety of configurations. A compact, hand-held package or a complete display can be assembled almost instantly, and can be folded up again just as quickly.

ADVERTISER: Generic
PRODUCER: Einson Freeman

This instant stacker display can be used in a variety of configurations. A compact, hand-held package or a complete display can be assembled almost instantly, and can be folded up again just as quickly.

ADVERTISER: Generic
PRODUCER: Einson Freeman

This instant stacker display can be used in a variety of configurations. A compact, hand-held package or a complete display can be assembled almost instantly, and can be folded up again just as quickly.

ADVERTISER: The Southland Corp
Wm W. Scott, Manager, Olympic Planning Committee
H. Douglas Thompson, Sports Coordinator, Olympic Planning Committee
PRODUCER: The Howard/Marlboro Group
Milton Merl, Designer

This free-standing merchandiser is designed to inform the consumer about the 7–11 convenience stores' participation in support for the Olympics, and gets him involved.

ADVERTISER: Generic

PRODUCER: Thomson-Leeds Co. Inc.

These literature holders come in two pieces, so they mail flat, and snap together for use. Best of all, in spite of their prestige appearance, their cost is less than most cardboard holders.

ADVERTISER: AT&T
PRODUCER: The Display Equation Inc.

Introducing a brand-new concept is not easy, especially when it must be done in a limited region. This free-standing demonstration unit combines the monitor, the terminal box, and the key-pad in a single unit that permits the customer to try the system. Pilfer-proofing of all elements has been done invisibly, with mechanical means.

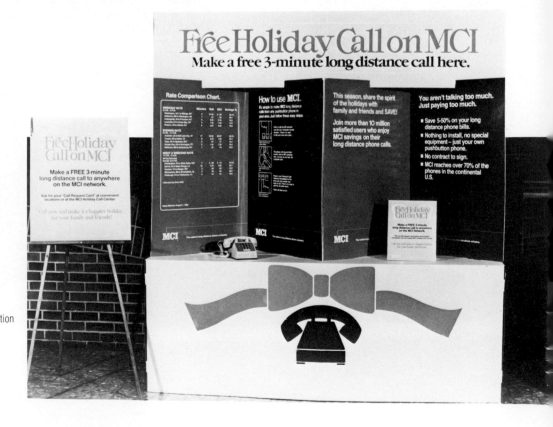

ADVERTISER: MCI Telecommunications Corp.
Timothy C. Cronin, Director of Advertising
William Buterbaugh, Senior Manager, Sales Promotion
PRODUCER: Burke Communications Industries Inc.

Designed for high traffic areas in shopping malls and department stores, this display was so successful during its initial Christmas showing that it has been extended and used during other major holiday periods. Bronze OMA 1983.

ADVERTISER: Pizza Hut Franchise Services
Larry Taylor, Manager Promotions, Sales
PRODUCER: KCS Industries Inc.

Membership in the Birthday Buddies Club, an on-going promotion at Pizza Hut, is solicited with this attractive display which can be placed on a counter or mounted to the wall. The graphics on the riser card attracts attention, and the copy explains how the club works. Cards are taken from the rack, filled out, and placed in the base, which is a replica of the restaurant and its familiar red roof. Bronze OMA 1983.

ADVERTISER: Long John Silver's
Dwight Shelton
PRODUCER: Einson Freeman
Gary Bobcik, Designer

The treasure chest tied in with the theme of this fast food chain,
involved children who wished to take a premium.

ADVERTISER: New Jersey Lottery Commission
William Mulcahy, Director of Marketing
PRODUCER: KCS Industries Inc.

This neon sign is clean and bright, designed to remind customers to buy lottery tickets. Its simplicity makes it stand out in the often crowded candy/stationery stores where most tickets are sold. Silver OMA 1983.

ADVERTISER: White Hen Pantry, Jewel Companies Inc.
Barbara Nosek, Advertising Manager
Judith Cihock, Promotion Supervisor
PRODUCER: Frank Mayer and Associates

This promotion kit included window streamers, tent cards, and counter packs, all designed for each franchisee to operate the promotion on an individual basis. Bronze OMA 1983.

ADVERTISER: Purolator Courier Corp.
James McCormick, Manager, Marketing and Sales Administration
Ron Yavorka, VP, Operations
PRODUCER: DCI Marketing

The drop box was designed to be a convenience to Purolator customers, but also a device to quicken pick-ups in large office buildings. To match building lobby decoration, the unit was offered in either brushed silver or brushed architectural bronze, with a choice of three different door coverings. The box is locked, with instructions and a pick-up schedule mounted under shatterproof glass on the top of the box. Bronze OMA 1983.

ADVERTISER: Hardee's Food System
William D. Cunningham, Director of Production Services
AGENCY: Lewis Advertising Inc.
PRODUCER: Southern Corrugated Box Co.
David Church, Designer

To back up a national promotion of a 3-D Adventure Meal box for children, this lobby display was prepared to show that the restaurant was participating. Bronze OMA 1983.

ADVERTISER: Morrison's Cafeteria
AGENCY: Creative Services
Tom Wood, Creative Director
John Antonio, Art Director
PRODUCER: Case-Hoyt/Atlanta

A life-size, realistic floorstand invites customers to try Morrison's for the best seafood in town. Bronze OMA 1983.

Advertisers

C

D

Producers

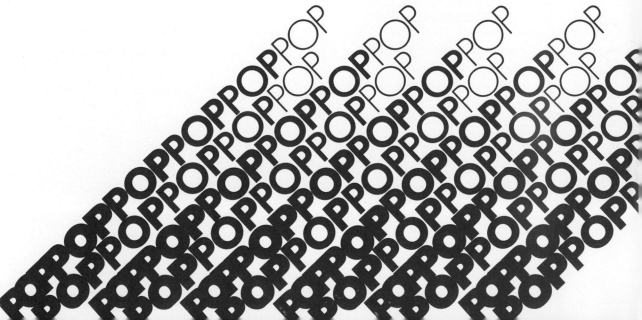